G000135005

CLEAR CUT

one woman's journey of life in the body

GINNY JORDAN

LANTERN BOOKS • NEW YORK
A DIVISION OF BOOKLIGHT INC.

2012
Lantern Books
128 Second Place
Brooklyn, NY 11231
www.lanternbooks.com

Printed in the United States of America

Library of Congress Cataloging-in-Publication Data

Jordan, Ginny.
Clear cut : one woman's journey of life in the body / Ginny Jordan.
p. cm.
ISBN 978-1-59056-316-8 (alk. paper)
1. Jordan, Ginny. 2. Sick—United States—Biography. 3. Sick—Psychology.
4. Women—Psychology. I. Title.
CT275.J675A3 2011
305.9'087—dc23
2011025549

2011
Publisher certification awarded by Green Press Initiative.
www.greenpressinitiative.org

"Our bodies are apt to be our autobiographies."

—FRANK GELETT BURGESS

"It's all awake in the darkness."

—W. S. MERWIN

⊞

Let something beautiful
Come out of me
Before my body lifts into fading light
Something tender and delicate
The way pelicans
Curl their wings behind their shoulders
Just before
Rising off the wave.

—GINNY JORDAN

Contents

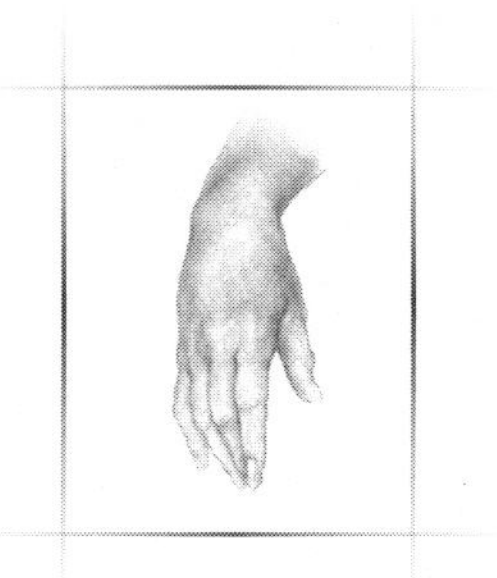

For my children, Taylor, Cameron, and Brooke,

and Max Regan

Prologue

MY BODY STARTS HEAVING. Exhaustion encases everything I do, even washing the kids' cereal bowls. It feels as though layers of thick gauze have wrapped themselves around the faces of my three children. A hardened grayness taking over the spaces between everything. Sealing the tissue between my ribs. Filling in the distance between the kitchen window and the soccer ball in the backyard.

One doctor thinks I am still caught in the fist of the mononucleosis I contracted in college; another tells me that giving birth to three children is enough to swell anyone's glands and break open these rivers of mucous. Infection after infection keeps me from my kids' tennis matches and class trips to Canyonlands in Utah. The fatigue gathers in my chest, leaving my arms heavy and my fingers numb. Daily headaches send me back to bed after breakfast. The words "chronic illness" move into my house, wandering the rooms, trying to steal parts of my body.

My thin, bare feet slide down the hall to wake up the children for school.

I have no idea what is happening.

. . .

My four brothers and I grow up in Perrysburg, a small town on the Maumee River just outside of Toledo, Ohio. Surrounded by cornfields, Perrysburg rests on swampland that was filled with snakes, wolves, wildcats, biting flies, and mosquitoes until farmers drained it and turned it into rich farmland. This small town spreads itself in coils along the Maumee. The river sucks off my sandals and pulls me in circles as I float on an old tire over its dark amber surface. The town has train tracks, small grocery stores, alleys, old dried quarries, and a rusted cannon commemorating the battle at Fort Meigs in 1813. On each suburban block stand green-trimmed houses that match my party shoes, the backyards guarded by huge Dutch elms. We enjoy weekend rib barbeques with the Smiths and the Balls and the Giffords with their kids, Sallie and Margaret and Libby, Chuck, and Whitney. On hot, humid nights, the smell of dead reeds rises from the river.

I become obsessed with the natural world and thoughts of the sea. Time seems to have huge gaps like the spaces between my fingers when I raise my hands to my face. I learn the names of trees—the ash, the mulberry, the buckeye—and they become *my* trees, as I attempt to make the neighborhood my own.

On Saturdays, I wear my zip-up red sweatshirt and tightrope-walk the railroad track along Front Street. I travel the distance of my imagination, taking my mind to white beaches in the Caribbean, to parrot fish with eyes the size of marbles. My legs are as thin as milkweeds. Mr. Dupree, my third-grade science teacher, lets me complete my final project outside barefoot, because he knows I love the earth.

Through the years, my body is something I carry with me. I fall to illness easily: ear infections, colds, flu, strep throat. Yet, every summer at our cabin, I find my toes on Cricket Island in the North Channel of Ontario. I fall in love with the birch trees and the slender canoes. After a cold swim to the point of Dawson, my body unfolds on the warmed flat rocks of the Canadian Shield. From my pinewood bed, the knotholes in the uninsulated cabin walls are portals into a landscape lined with spruce, pine, and oak—a channel deep enough for big oared ships, a wooden swimming raft waiting for me to jump. I know I am lucky to sit at a table and eat fresh blueberry muffins, to sleep under a thick wool blanket and watch the sun rise out of the collar of Stobie Creek. Here my body finds itself.

The day I see Roger, he is wearing torn blue jeans with a handmade, black-and-gray wool satchel slung over his chest. *This man is my future*, I say to myself. We pledge to heal each other of every wound.

Above my college door hangs a piece of cardboard that notes in black magic marker the wisdom of Apollo—"Know thyself"—just like the one above Carl Jung's door. I graduate with a degree in psychology and find a future as a psychotherapist. I am not afraid of the broken parts of other people. I explore dreams and the mysterious art of interpretation as a way of guiding others into their own interiors.

Roger and I drive in search of a new home, a place free enough for our eighty-pound Komondor dog, Tai, and a home in which to raise children. We stake our claim in Boulder, Colorado, cinched against the foothills of the Rocky Mountains. Eleven months after our wedding—on Monday, December 27th, 1978—I give birth to my son Taylor. Somehow I know my entire twenty-five years of life has been pitched for this. Taylor tacks toward the tide of my voice; his tiny hand folds into mine. Twenty months later, Cameron is born. Six years later, comes Brooke.

We take the children to Disney World for vacation. As I lie at night in the hotel where thousands of other parents have slept I feel so exhausted it's as if a cinder block is sitting on my chest. I know something is wrong.

Three weeks later, I find I have cancer. From this moment, everything changes. I start to forego parts of my body and my children take baths with a one-breasted mother. I lose my dignity and my appetite. I shake so hard at night that I escape to the bathroom and fall asleep curled on my left side on the white wool carpet. Brooke starts to make angels out of Kleenex, folding two triangles into wings, and plays hospital with her sick dolls. My body becomes the stranger at the door, someone I have to take care of and feed, but who is not *me*. My body starts to live outside of me.

I endure chemotherapy and try to continue to see clients, to focus on the sorrow of others. I greet everyone at the door with the extra pep required to make cancer into my teacher. My work is a relief from the monotony of chugging vitamins and fresh vegetable juices. I rely on kindness. Before she dies, my friend Treya tells me that chemo is *a soul killer*. An average day is when a baked potato with sour cream staves off the nausea; a bad day is when my feet feel like someone poured hot liquid mercury over them; a good day is when I have the energy to brush Cameron's hair. 

A year and a half after finding the lump, I leave for Assisi, Italy. I want to follow in the footsteps of St. Francis. My toes cling to his rope sandals. I want to know how to walk with scars.

I meet Italians who love to sit in the piazzas and tell stories about their mothers' cooking. I am trying to practice living, to rely on a body to recover what it is losing. But I lose faith in small things. On a day outing to Gubbio, the battery in my watch dies and I have no idea where to get a new one.

On the journey from Assisi to Florence, vertigo flings me to the floor of the train. My right ear tortures me with a loud ringing. I see the mouths of the passengers above me and they seem like cartoons. I can't hear a word. The train windows grow larger and the landscape beyond flips over so that the tops of trees seem to fall into my mouth.

I am diagnosed with Ménière's disease, a condition that joins me with my mother and grandmother, who both suffered the symptoms of hearing loss and ear-ringing for years, although neither experienced such violent vertigo. The attacks come when I least expect them: at the movies, in the car driving home from Taylor's class play, while I am in my closet hanging up my dress.

Our family life reorganizes around Sick Mommy—who has an attack and can't move her head, not even an inch, and who vomits for nine solid hours. I become Unpredictable Mommy, who can't remember if she sent the check for soccer league. I become Sad Mommy, who cries when she can't find her blue ballet-style shoes. I become Absent Mommy: Taylor makes the winning three-point shot without me. I fall asleep without being present to sense relaxation come over me. Roger cups his sensitive hands on the back of my skull to help let the light in. Neither one of us knows what to do.

Two years later, the surgeon drills a half-dollar-sized hole into my skull, behind my ear, to thread a tiny valve into my inner ear. For eight weeks, I sleep sitting upright so the valve won't dislodge. I cheat and slide down the pillows stacked like giant marshmallows. Eventually, my bedroom stops revolving or turning upside down and I can drive the children to the Spring Fair. Eventually, I can lean over and tie my tennis shoes without being afraid of falling over.

But it does not end. Three years after this, I start having drop attacks. The floor slams into me so fast it feels as though a bullet has blasted into my head. Terrified, I crawl on my hands and knees to the kitchen. This time, they inject toxic drugs into my inner ear and I lose my balance on the right side. I lose my hearing on the right side. I lose my temper on the right side. Everything—the hall, the sink, the legs of my desk—goes sideways. I have to learn to walk again.

A year later, friends help me climb Huayna Picchu, the mountain facing Machu Picchu, and I fall in love with Peru's textures and shapes, rivers and mountains, and people. I am able to raft the Grand Canyon. I am able to swim in the North Channel and canoe at night.

I return to school and get an MFA in poetry. I stay up late and study the language of Blake, Dickinson, and Emerson. These poets mess up the bed with their tossing and turning. Everyone's voice is thoroughly loud and brilliantly clear.

Brooke, now sixteen, and Cameron, twenty-two, both have a deep sensitivity to the HIV epidemic in Africa. My friend Charles, who is a doctor, and his wife, Torkin, invite us to come to Uganda to work in a refugee camp and visit orphanages. I begin to study the face of suffering. How is it possible that so many of these women still have some light in their eyes when they tell me how the rebel army stole their sons right out of their arms? This is when I learn that taking suffering personally is an act of violence. Toward myself. This is when I stop thinking of *my* cancer, as if I own this thing. Like my purse or my dress.

I have the privilege to travel big distances: Morocco, Tasmania, Malta, Elba, Peru, and Africa again. I want to walk the landscapes of a life and see how loss is measured. I yearn to meet people exactly where they are: on the cold earth in a hut in the Andes, on the dry red soil of an African house made of old tin scraps. I take dozens of pairs of eyeglasses. I want to give them parts of their body back. The old village shaman can now read his cherished text on plant medicine, which his father gave him.

. . .

Boulder starts feeling like a place to have mammograms. I get my six-month checkup with my oncologist, receive acupuncture. Vigilance becomes my death eater.

Seventeen years after my first biopsy, the doctor calls to tell me the white calcifications on my mammogram are starting to look like a constellation. Another biopsy. The left side. The doctor nets one. *That's all we need*, he says. Another body part goes. My left breast.

This time I stay with the rest of my body, coach it through the fear of anesthesia. Just like the crab apple tree by the front door, I seem to know what it is to have a harvest, then drop all my leaves. The dead have passed through me and I am still alive. This time they catch the cancer before it infiltrates. This time I know how to touch my own chest.

Roger moves to California and our hearts sink. Our marriage formed when we were so young; our differences become an abyss of unhappiness. I break from grief. I replay thousands of hours of conversation: in the studio, in the hot tub, at the basketball game, late at night in bed. I hear the way his voice rises at the end of each sentence, waiting for me to join. Thirty years of space and word uncoupling.

This time in my recovery bed I try to say goodbye to a body I grew up with. To a man I made love with. To three children I raised and who are now gone from home. I put myself to bed at night.

How do I come toward myself? What does it mean to eat alone at the head of the old farmhouse table we bought in Santa Fe? A friend asks if this is like eating with ghosts. I tell her I think ghosts are living in the space between where my breasts were. The empty chairs and beds.

A year later there are more medical tests. There are my father's bad genes and my bad genes. Another body part needs to go. My ovaries.

This time I say goodbye alone.

In the quiet of my home I start to mark the lost and found. I look in the deep and dark places inside and outside my body. Below the cavity of my absent breasts are thousands of other breastless women. In the hole of flesh on my right thigh where a bad mole was rooted out I find my friend Cindy's husband, who died of a melanoma. I find my grandmother in my right ear, my father in my leg, Dr. Smith's hand in my own palm. I start to tag parts, whether mine or those of others. I use little yellow stickies and start to ask questions. How does hair speak, exactly? Is each strand a letter that when combed together makes a story? Do absent breasts speak to chest walls? Does my inner ear talk to my brain to keep me upright? Does my father's cancerous leg still have a place in the world? Does the human heart time its beat to loss?

I lay out my right breast, hair, hand, left breast, my father's leg and my leg, my vagina, my right ear, heart, and ovaries. I bow to each of them and begin. I pledge to make them feel beautiful.

I pledge to them I will be true.

1

Right Breast

I AM SO TIRED I can barely move. My legs feel like they are encased in wet cement. The doctor says I need to rest. *After all, you have three young children*, he says.

In the spring, Roger and I take the kids to Disney World: the duty of any parent. I lie immobile on a hard bed. My dreams push hard against my forehead. On April 16th—one week later and the day after I notice the first crocus by the back door—a dream breaks through:

> Two overly enthusiastic workshops leaders have given me a special assignment. I am told to name something, stop something. Suddenly I am flying very low over the surface of the earth. I see a waterfall of billions of cells pouring off the beautiful curve

of the planet. I have to stop it. I raise my arms to the heavens, imploring a great power to pass through me. A bolt of lightning shoots into the crown of my head, forcing my long blond hair to stand straight on end. Electric blue light fires out of my hands across a blackened abyss.

I name DEATH and collapse onto the floor.

There is little left of me.

Like a Japanese block print, the waterfall leans over the earth, frozen in its tracks: a wave form of horror. I don't even have the energy to marvel. A silent knowing spreads through my body. Deep inside, I collapse under the weight of what feels like doom. Instead, I decide that my dream means I am preparing for a major transformation: something noble and challenging or, at least, hard work.

What am I supposed to stop?

A month after the dream I call The Big One, the morning after I plant lettuce seeds in the garden, I sweep my hands over my breasts. It is a Sunday morning, and I am luxuriating in bed with Roger and Brooke. I find a lump the size of a BB in my right breast just above the nipple. *Roger, feel this.* He does, and confirms that he can feel it, too. It is here: a foreign object, a misplaced seed.

The tears start later in the morning after I call my doctor friend Charles. He takes me seriously. He wants to stop by on the way down the mountain so he can feel the lump himself. The taste of bile spills into my throat. Taylor has a meltdown because he can't find his basketball, and Roger doesn't know how to take my hand.

I start sliding down the chute of being a patient: the referrals, my first mammogram. I sit in the waiting room with other women who are older. My friend Julie, a doctor, calls me in: *It looks suspicious*, she says. I am to see Dr. Brenton. He looks like my father, with his kind blue eyes and receding hairline. His fingers point to a round grayish spot on the x-ray film. *Do you see all these white dots inside? They are called* calcifications.

I clean the linen closet. I throw away any sheets and tablecloths that have little holes. When I talk to the kids, my voice sounds as though the syllables are divorced from the words, as though complete sentences are finishing themselves above my head and floating out my mouth. I sleep on my left side, my back facing away from the plateglass window. Stars. Night. Moon. Are all too big for me. I start to burrow. Into the sheets. Into the book on bird migration. Into the corner of the shower.

My friend Karen tells me that a biopsy is a piece of cake. *You'll be awake. You'll know everything that is going on.* She means to comfort me. But I don't want to know *everything*.

The nurse draws a big X on my right breast with a red magic marker. It smells like new onions. I look down at my breast and pull myself further inside. The operating room is cold and silent. The cylindrical barrel lights look like they are hanging a thousand feet above me. I hear feet shuffling in paper booties nearby. Shining knives lie in order on the tray next to me like little bayonets. Dr. Brenton raises his eyes above me and tells me he is going to start.

Ready?

I nod my head with forced bravery, like a five-year-old being asked if she is ready for her tetanus shot. The radio is playing. One of the nurses takes my hand and squeezes it. I close my eyes and try to go somewhere else: first to the dock on Cricket Island, then to the bench on the bank of Left Hand Creek. I look for the deep green in Roger's eyes.

I hear Dr. Brenton ask for the vessel cauterizer. He tells me he's got the section he wants. I turn and watch a nurse place a piece of flesh in a tube balanced gently in the palm of her hand. She heads out the door. The IV beeps and Dr. Brenton asks for gauze. A phone rings and the nurse answers. *Good, thank you for being so quick.* I envision some pale pathologist hovering over his microscope, calling from the bowels of the hospital.

I'm sorry, Dr. Brenton says slowly, deliberately, to me. *It's malignant.*

I try to break it down. MA-LIG-NANT. The curl of the tongue at the roof of the mouth; the last syllable flicking against the back of the teeth.

Dr. Brenton tells me there are only a few more stitches, although the procedure might take a moment longer to complete. *It's delicate around the nipple,* he says. His breath labors behind the paper mask squeezed tight against his nose. A tear starts to fall and make its way down my cheek into the corner of my mouth. My shoulder blades pinch themselves around the back of my neck. The lights are too bright.

Malignancy has entered my body, like a long-lost relative that has always wanted a room in my house. In my dreams over the last year, malignancy has been calling me: *I am coming*. Sometimes it was a hungry mountain lion, sometimes a man with black horns. I ask myself, *Malignant equals cancer equals what?*

I turn and stare at the top of the IV bag, a blue swirl of fluid attached to a pole, connected to my wrist, linked to my blood. Umbilicus. Meanwhile, the nurse is trying to be kind. *Do you want another heated blanket?* she asks. Valium protects me: a foot-thick viscous padding wrapped around my torso. I drift to the back of the room, near the automatic doors, toward where Roger and my friend Suzanne are sitting in the waiting room, reading the Monday edition of *The New York Times*. I want to tell them first, with the quiet and clear voice that comes with fact. *This is how it is*.

When I do, Roger cries without a sound, wetting his silver-gray silk shirt. Suzanne tells me with certainty: *We can do this*. She doesn't know that, while Dr. Brenton threads the last stitches, I am already telling myself the same things, stitching myself together with conviction and hope.

My dream told me to name something, to stop something. I know as well as I know the length of my own fingers that my cells are pouring off the earth. Fast. I solemnly say to the void, *Take my breast*. There is no time. The tumor is 2.5 cm, the size of the tip of my baby finger. Progesterone and estrogen sensitive.

The biopsy site burns. I fall asleep with a bag of frozen peas over my stitches.

Roger and I tell the kids, just enough. Taylor is nine, Cameron is seven, and Brooke is two. For Brooke, we call it a *big owie*. For Taylor and Cameron, we name it: *breast cancer*. But, we say, it is different from what happened to Karen or Treya. It is earlier. Better.

At ten a.m. on Wednesday, May 24th, Dr. Brenton, with Dr. Carpenter assisting, at Boulder Community Hospital, will take my breast. A mastectomy—the surgical removal of the breast. A lymphadenectomy, the surgical removal of lymph nodes.

There must be a hundred thousand ways to die. For me, the absolute worst is death from anesthesia. When I think of it, it's as if I am on a plane going down over the sea, submerged in cold water, unable to break through the thick ice. Frozen to death. I start shaking at night from the thought of it—the finality of it. Three young children left behind, and their mommy dead at the bottom of the ocean.

I research the odds. The risk of death from commercial flying is one in ten million. If the average flying time is two hours, then five will die per one hundred million hours of exposure. The risk of preventable death from anesthesia is one in a hundred thousand. If the average anesthesia lasts two hours, then five hundred will die per one hundred million hours of exposure. Anesthesia is not as safe as flying in an airplane.

The white terror of absence follows me. It accompanies me as I rock Brooke to sleep. It follows me to the bathroom at three a.m., as I kneel on the floor with my face in my hands. It joins me in the laundry room as I try to rub out the grass stains on Taylor's soccer shorts. The night before surgery, I dream of a huge white stallion pawing the ground in a corral. He wants out, and starts to spin in very tight circles, gathering speed. Finally, he shoots himself toward the railing and jumps. I watch him storm over the open field, dust clouds exploding out of the backs of his hooves. I smile and say to myself, *He's done it.*

I'm doing it.

I'll be home soon.

The young nurse attaches the clear blue wristband to my left wrist, because, she tells me, *your surgery is on the right.* She takes me to my room on the fourth floor, where I can see the foothills of the Rockies from both windows. My cotton gown is mint green. I note the snacks in paper bags, the admission papers stacked on the swinging, fake-wood table. As she walks out of the room she smiles. *It's the nicest room in the inn*, she says.

The medical team attempts to get an IV in four times. Blood is spilled and I cry. I scan the nurse's face for a sign of compassion. She is my bridge.

Can I close my eyes now?

My legs are filling with water. Roger comes in to tell me they are ready. Dr. Brenton has finished his coffee. The nurse asks me to lie down so I can be wheeled out.

We can't have you falling out of bed, can we?

I ask for a few minutes. I take Roger into the hospital bathroom, wheeling my IV pole, the plastic tubing looped over my arm. A saline sea courses through my veins, joining my life to the great waters. There is some safety in this connection. I take my husband's face firmly in my hands and look into his sad eyes. *If I don't make it, you must give everything you have in you, I mean everything, to the kids*. I don't know how to say, *Love them as I would.* I can't breathe. I try to swallow, but my throat feels like it is full of rocks.

My cotton gown is loose at the back. *Rog, please tie me up*.

Roger drapes a warm blanket over my body and leans over to say goodbye. *Hang in, my Amazonian wife. Sweet dreams*.

The technician unlocks the brake and gives my bed a push. I am the warrior now. Soon enough, the great white foam races headlong into my mouth.

When I wake, I see that a large glossy picture of a white horse has been taped to the ceiling above my head. The thin edges of scotch tape cross three corners, while the bottom-left corner curls up on its own. My friend Fleur must have done this while I was asleep. This is friendship.

It's as if I am coming from below. My chest feels like the skin of a drum stretched tight. I try to push my breath through a wall of flesh to get my chest to rise, to fill the hole of my empty breast. I ask the nurse for more pain medicine and float between layers of thick clouds and the acid smell of burnt flesh.

Dr. Brenton enters my room and takes my hand. He reports that everything went well. *You must be a swimmer*, he says. *The muscles in your armpits are so strong.* He tells me he wrestled twenty-two lymph nodes out of the lower channels. He hands Roger the preliminary pathology report. Two nodes have cancer cells: *Poor margins*, he explains, *more aggressive than the original tumor. You will definitely have to do chemo*.

I know.

I want to find out where my breast went, after they sliced off my nipple and cut my breast into sections and spread the cells onto slides. Who exactly touched it? Were the nurse's nails painted red under her latex gloves? Or were they men who sliced up my breast? Did they talk about their children or the TV show they saw the previous night while they filleted a part of my body? Did they wonder who the woman was who belonged to this breast—whether she was a soccer mom, a good cook? Did they know she is only thirty-five?

When I finally arrive home, I take the risk to look. I carefully pull the tape off and unwrap the bandages, avoiding the drain tubes that stick out of my chest. The distance between my eyes and my sternum feels like the length of my driveway. The right side of my chest is so flat that I can see my toes. The line of stitches is so perfectly straight I think the doctor must have used a ruler. I touch the little breaks on my skin, feeling for any remains of my breast. It is like digging through ashes with a stick after a fire. I press my fingertips in between the stitches for anything soft.

Nothing.

It takes me an hour to cry. *Goodbye*. I whisper, *Goodbye*.

It's time for Brooke's bath. My arms feel leaden as I get into the tub and lift her onto my lap. We are performing the usual ritual. We float four yellow plastic duckies and wind up the whale. I make waves with my hands, sink down, and lean back in the tub. I have no hair to cushion the back of my head. I close my eyes and drift into her baby sounds. My two-year-old, my round Buddha child, puttering and blowing. Brooke turns around and spontaneously hugs me, wrapping her arms around my neck. She tells me she doesn't want to be a big girl.

Why not?

She tells me that when she gets to be a big girl she will have an *owie* like mine. She pulls on her tiny nipples, making boat noises, and throws her head back and laughs. I sink down lower, my heart crushed.

Brookie, this is my owie, not yours.

My one breast floats. It swings from side to side, rests, then dips under the surface and bounces back up. Dr. Sitarik tells me my remaining breast has very dense tissue, which is why it has so many fibrous cysts. He doesn't know it can float. He doesn't know how happy it is to set sail on its own. The bliss of having one left.

My friend Alexa writes:

> You should see the cherry trees in bloom. My backyard is a sea of pink blossoms. Next year you will be well enough to come to Washington to see for yourself. Terry just got a new job at the bank closer to home. He told me to tell you he has always thought you were beautiful, breasts or not. At dinner we all talk about how brave you are.

I look at the pine tree outside the bedroom window. The one I call The Great Mother. She never moved during my home labor with Brooke. She held me in her branches and said, *You can do this*. I decide not to go to Washington to see the cherry trees blossom. Next spring, I'll kneel here and admire how the pine needles twirl in the rain.

A girlfriend takes me to the cranberry-colored house across from the hospital to shop for a prosthesis. A nurse in the hospital tells me that the owner is very nice and professional and I can try the pieces on in the comfort of her home. I still hold my right arm close to my chest, as if I were a bird with a wounded wing. The pain under my armpit reaches deep into a black hole of loss. I try hard to do the exercises:

> Reach for the top shelf for the can of tuna fish.
> Squeeze the rubber ball a hundred times before bed.
> Lean over and touch my toes.
> Walk my fingers up the wall.
> Put my bra on by myself by fastening the hooks behind me.
> Clasp a necklace behind my neck.

I add: Hug my children at least three times a day.

I remember the pre-teen in me, fervently pressing her palms together, elbows out. Trying to swell my breast buds into full bloom. The training bras I begged my mother to buy.

Sarah takes me into her pantry filled with shelves of boxes with labels of breast sizes: left 32, right 32, left 34, right 34, left 36, right 36, left 38, right 38, left 40, right 40. I am scanning for where she has put the cans of tomato soup and jars of almonds and paper plates, but I only see breasts.

The most common construction is silicone gel in a plastic skin, Sarah explains. *These are symmetrical shapes, the teardrop and the triangle. The asymmetrical shape is called* The Tail of Spence. *This is when you have a lot of breast tissue coursing toward your armpit.*

Sarah gently places in my hand prostheses that stick to the chest wall and are to be used without a bra. There are heavy ones that feel like real breasts; light ones with breathable, vented cotton backs to be used for sports; soft ones with the nipple built in; firmer ones with attachable nipples. I cup the 34 B soft one in my hand and weigh it with a measure that I have never learned. How much exactly did my breast weigh? As much as my tennis shoe? My hairbrush?

I leave the box with Sarah and go home with my prosthesis in my coat pocket.

When I slide my prosthesis into my bra, I turn sideways to check. Does the right side look like the left? Too low? Too high? My t-shirt hugs my chest for a world that looks at woman's breasts: upright and perky. Would someone be able to tell when I hugged them that one side is a pretense?

When I pull up Brooke's socks, I travel the distance to her wedding day and adjust her veil just like I am always adjusting my prosthesis to land level across my chest. When I fiddle with Taylor's purple velvet cap, his costume in the Shakespeare play, my prosthesis raises out of my bra cup as if it were an escaped prisoner. I imbue my prosthesis with its own life and wonder if it knows it is a replacement.

I look in the dictionary for the word *asymmetry*: a relation between two things where the first has a relation to the second but the second cannot have the same relation to the first.

I think about the God-given design of pairs and the partnerships of the body: eyes, nostrils, lips, ears, tonsils, lungs, breasts, kidneys, arms, elbows, hands, hip bones, ovaries, legs, knees, feet.

I recall how my mother, arranging flowers in an amethyst glass vase, once told me that a successful arrangement, one that will *make an impression* and not just stand there looking like a refugee, had to have symmetry. She cut the stem of a peach-colored iris and put it in the vase so it leaned away from the other one. *Let them enhance each other*, she intoned.

I remember my father sitting on his favorite chocolate-brown leather couch with his two feet on the coffee table. Symmetry. He tells me of a great company in New York City that makes the lifts for all his right shoes. He is wearing the newest ones, a pair of Top-Siders. He says the company had to add another inch onto the existing three inches because he can't hold the chiropractic adjustments for much longer than a week. The pressure on his good hip is too great. His voice lilts with pride. *Twenty-five more pounds on the left side*, he brags. The doctors wanted to amputate his right leg when they found cancer in his hip socket. But my father was adamant: *If I can't fish, I can't live.* He opts for option B—cut out the tumor, live in a full body cast for six months, and *pray like hell* that enough scar tissue forms so he can get in and out of boats.

. . .

I read that one in two hundred women have more than two breasts, a condition called *polymastia.* This includes extra nipples or little breast buds without nipples. In 1886, a medical academic discovered a Polish woman who had five pairs of lactating breasts. Julia, the mother of the Roman emperor Alexander Severus, was reportedly many-breasted. Ann Boleyn, Henry VIII's doomed wife, was said to have three—the third above the right breast, near the armpit. Like me: one in two hundred. I remember the shock of milk dripping out of the little mound of flesh near my right armpit when I began lactating for Taylor. That little extra nipple is cut out with my breast. *Dangerous*, Dr. Brenton mutters when he examines me.

So much depends on my remaining left breast. I switch sides of the bed with Roger so I can roll over on it, my nipple cupped in the Egyptian cotton sheet.

On my bedside table, the yellow roses are just opening.

Peggy asks me to the movies, and her twenty-something male roommate tells me the film is great. Feeling housebound all day, we break out. When the main characters joke in the movie about breasts, I cringe. *Great tits*, the wannabe-sexy cowboy says to his buddy. They laugh a raunchy, guttural blast. I wonder how many women in the theater are sinking into their seats? Are their boyfriends or husbands taking their hand? I grab the armrests on my seat, as if I am riding a wild horse. I wonder if these women are checking their breasts under their sweaters, as if to pat an old friend, as if to say *Great chest*: a kind of warrior's greeting, a flag raising.

The cowboy blabs on and on about the woman's great body, how he wants to bury his head in her jugs and drink until the cows come in. All I can think of are other sources of milk and pastures I'll never walk. My mother tells me I was allergic to cow's milk and that she never considered breast-feeding, of how her generation thought *the whole thing embarrassing*.

I wonder if the men in the movie theater would lust over breasts if they weren't peeking out from under a lacy bra. Isn't this *really* the appeal, the old games of catch-me-if-you-can and peek-a-boo? I can't focus on anything but cleavage, since that's all they seem to be giving us in this movie: the deep plunge, the cluster of grapes.

A woman in the row in front of us stirs. She holds her breasts under her crossed arms, oblivious to the way they swing out anyway. I remember in Africa how the women roll their babies from their backs onto their exposed breasts. How I watched a breast-feeding woman pull up her red cotton shirt and tuck it around her neck like a beautiful necklace.

The right side of my chest looks like a ghostly crater on the moon, concave and strangely ephemeral. It's been so long since I felt the valley of cleavage that collects a pool of sweat or the channel my baby's hand slides down while nursing dreamily. In high school, I would walk around with a Hershey's kiss between my breasts to see how long it took to melt. Once, I forgot about my little experiment until the end of biology class, when I felt a rivulet making its way toward my belly button. I lifted up my shirt to see a design between my breasts with a perfect chocolate line. A dragonfly with a long, beautiful tail.

Finally, we line up to leave the theater, the men tipsy and titillated. I look into a few women's eyes, hooded in the dark. I can't read their shame. We are careful not to bump into each other, careful not to feel anyone else's breasts rub against our heavy coats.

I'm tired of talking about breasts. My friend Molly tells me she is *over it*. She has hers *lopped off*. *I won't die like my mother*. I have never heard her speak of them since. No morning talks about prostheses, or bathing suits, or tank tops, or her husband's needs. Besides, she has finished nursing three children. *Lucky*, she says. *I'm lucky*.

She tells me she had the smell of liniment on her hands for years after watching her mother die.

On a writing retreat in Santa Fe, Dianne, a sixtyish, dark-haired woman in a long turquoise skirt, corners me at the door of my newly rented house. In five minutes, she spills the gist of her life story. Divorced from a famous actor, she is burnt out on the Hollywood scene. She confides that she prefers her bohemian-style house in Santa Fe. She tells me that the greatest achievement of her life is her daughter Sophia. *We are attached at the hip bone*, she announces.

Squeezing behind me into the kitchen, Dianne explains that she is taking a retreat herself, having just gone through six months of treatment for breast cancer. In the tiny living room, she tells me eagerly that her beautiful daughter is in the middle of a horrible divorce and had a serious case of breast cancer four years ago. I respond with niceties. *I've been there, too.*

She invites me over for a glass of wine. *Anytime.*

Two days later, I find a note pinned under my windshield wiper: *Call me. My daughter has had a reoccurrence.* I stuff the note in my purse and head out to yoga class. I flash on Brooke at thirteen leaping down the bedroom hall in a sleeveless white dress: her breasts, her flood of hormones, her freedom, her joy. My joy. How she wraps a peacock-blue boa around her neck for all of us to admire.

The tears start as I pull out of the driveway.

At dinner, I tell Fleur the story and rant. *Women are trying so hard, and we are beautiful and sincere and we have children to raise, we can't make our lives about IVs and bald doctors and trying to remember the color of our hair and new drug cocktails. We can't spend hours on the phone or be driven to appointments to sit in waiting rooms with stale air. We can't lie on metal tables being examined by tired nurses or attend support groups in the basements of hospitals. We can't squander our nights in the bathroom throwing up.*

I throw my napkin down. *This has got to end.*

2
HAIR

IN THE END I decide to cut it short.

I wish I had the correct ritual object—like the Eskimo, who use the lower teeth of the Greenland shark to cut their hair. I choose a pair of kitchen scissors. I have never cut my own hair. I stand in front of the mirror above my bureau in the closet. As I reach behind to grab my long ponytail, I think of cavemen dragging their women; of Rapunzel who never suspected her long tresses would betray her; of Joan of Arc shaking before she chopped off her hair in order to fit her head into a knight's helmet. I hold the scissors above my head. My hand trembles. I cut my entire ponytail as a hara-kiri and discover a twelve-inch clump of hair in my palm held together by a plastic tortoise shell clasp. It is another initiation. The mirror blurs as I cry. A thin-sounding wail fills my mouth.

It happens like everyone says. First, a few strands come off in my hand when I push my hair off my forehead. Then the brush pulls out clods, like tumbleweed caught in wire. Quarter-sized bald patches appear behind my ear. I am becoming someone I don't know. My DNA lies on the cotton lavender pillowcase: my final strands of hair, shining against a purple field, dead and naked.

I inherited the color from my father, who was always called Whitey. I recall my father touching my hair, brushing his arm against it when he carried me to the car. And how he gently combed it after a bath and shampoo and organized the curls to the sides, making a perfect part with the black plastic comb. I remember his hard brown leather suitcase standing at the door, announcing that he was leaving for another sales trip. He would lean over to hug me, his hair separated in thin strips and glistening with gel. He smelled like the oak trees in the front yard after the rain.

My mother's dark hair is neat and mysterious. On Wednesday afternoons, she disappears to the beauty parlor to have it washed and rolled. She has lost the confidence of her own hands. I imagine a woman named Madeline, with a husky voice and large pendulous breasts—all red lipstick, flying hands, and earth—talking while she tips my mother's head back into the white basin. My mother wears a slippery black, curtain-like smock pulled tight across her throat. An ivory plastic chandelier hangs above her head, and she closes her eyes as the other ladies chat, their stubby, high-heeled shoes swinging back and forth, one hooked over the other. When my mother comes home, she unloads the groceries and sings to herself under her breath. Her dark hair is brushed smooth around her face.

When I am six years old, my mother takes me to the salon after school to pick up a new hairbrush. The salon is painted a deep rose color, its windows trimmed in white, and tucked behind the bank like a second-class citizen. It stinks of gasoline. My mother explains that this is what hair spray smells like, at first. *After it wears off*, she tells me, *your hair turns to the perfume of roses*. The receptionist, a thin elderly woman with perfectly set large, white curls, hands me a brown brush with black bristles. My mother is silent on the way home, lost in her reverie of scent. In the back seat I twirl her brush like a baton.

I love brushes, the way they make silk happen, but I hate brushing my own hair. After all, I don't have an older sister who loves sparkled clips and bows or prances around the house swinging her mane this way and that. My brothers aren't going to brush my hair a hundred times each night or teach me the attitudes of hair. Instead, I dream three nights before Christmas that Santa gives me a vanity set, a table covered in a pale pink-and-white gauzy skirting. On the glass top sits a gold-plated comb, its weight light in my hand. Sure enough, on Christmas Day, as I race down the long green-carpeted staircase, I catch a glimpse of something shining in the corner of the den: my very own vanity set. Overnight, I am more beautiful to myself.

I learn that my hair is a *feature*. Everyone seems to mention it or pat it or smell it. When my mother introduces me to her friends, she teasingly tells them that I got my coloring from her. I try to figure out the advantages to being blond. My brother Deke tells me a joke. *Why did the blonde climb the glass wall?* He doesn't wait for me to guess. *To see the other side*. I try to figure out the disadvantages.

When I am sitting, a shy twelve-year-old, at the booth at Houck's drugstore drinking a cherry Coke, a friend of my mother greets me as Virginia, though I can't remember her name. Her hands, a tangle of blue veins and large brown spots, move through my hair. She extols its beauty and asks if it's natural. I don't want her hands in my hair. I walk her over to the hair-care section and I point to a Revlon package that looks like a match. The color is called Simply Blond. So I'm not platinum blond, ash blond, or towhead; I'm not a sandy, dirty, dishwater, or a strawberry blonde. I am Simply Blond. My mother's friend and I exchange knowing looks, as if we are in on the Great Woman's Secret. *We must do all that we can*, she says.

When I am a teenager, I am referred to not just as the "Welles girl," but also as the "blond babe," and my father loves me for it. I learn to flash my hair with a quick turn on my heels. I find ways to hide my eyes in its folds, as if something exotic lies beneath. It's a game of dare. The romance of hair becomes me. I learn how to be coy.

One day in the library at school, while I'm examining my hair for split ends, a ninth-grade boy walks over. He's very tall, with a pinched face that looks like the snout of my neighbor's dog. He pulls a pair of scissors out of his book bag and asks if I need a haircut. Does this mean he likes me? Terrified, I bury my long hair in my book, *The Last of the Mohicans*, and start thinking about how it would feel to be scalped. What does it mean to possess someone by stealing her hair? My suitor flees to math class.

Girls chat in the locker room. *Why are some girls fair-haired with jet-black pubic hair? Does this mean eventually their light brown hair will turn black?* I wonder about the prophesies of the body. I start to examine my fingernails and the tiny folds on my hands for predictions of the woman I may become. That night in the bathtub, I pull and separate the new coils of blond pubic hair, as if to discover that there is no going back.

How is a woman made?

In college, I find myself on a campus with two hundred students, all poets and idealists. We are raised on meals of tofu and adzuki beans. We love our tie-dyed bedspreads and experiential education. I study with the mythologist Jean Houston and spiritual teacher Ram Dass and wear the same brown corduroy pants every day. My hair transforms itself from a crown of status into something chaotic. We are trying to make a different kind of statement. *We don't care, we hate war*, our generation chants.

I grow my hair down to my butt and stride across the commons with two hundred other hippies to say something to ourselves and the world. I don't care. I have never seen so much hair gathered in one place: afros high enough to catch blossoms from the orange groves; men's hair long enough to swing from; women's hair dull and unkempt, nests for doves of peace. We don't care. We're interested in higher things than grooming.

In late fall of my sophomore year, I spy a beautiful, six-foot-five-inches-tall man striding across the quad, wearing torn jeans. He's one of the few men with short hair and the skin on his face is as soft as a newborn's. In our white t-shirts we slide across the quad after a torrential thunderstorm, our hair plastered to our necks. We read *Siddhartha* late at night. The hair on his big toe is twirled like a wreath. I play Laura Nyro on the record player and sing to him with a blue plastic comb for a microphone. His name is Roger, but for a few friends his nickname is Tree. Some nights I hold on to him, and my body takes on the language of leaves.

In my senior year, I decide to do something with my long hair, a bid for glamour. I find the salon in Los Angeles where Susan Sarandon gets her hair done and give my hair into the hands of the emaciated, hyperactive Johnny, whose jet-black hair is parted in the middle, with the left side four inches higher than the right. *Do what you want*, I tell him. I'm not sure I mean it, but I close my eyes and drift toward a place where I'm someone new—as if I had long legs and could step into high heels and sophisticated artist talk. When I open my eyes I see a woman chopped into a concept. I want to cry. Thankfully, only a few friends ask where my hair went.

Whatever, I shrug. Hair grows seven inches per year. And each hair grows for six years before falling out. I calculate: if I don't cut it, my hair will be below my shoulders before Christmas and three and a half feet long by the time I am twenty-five. *By that time*, I tell myself, *I will have untamed myself*.

On my wedding day, I perm my hair into tight curls. A spray of white freesia tucked behind my ear falls to the floor on the way down the aisle.

Brooke is my only child born with hair. She has a downy blond fuzz with longer pieces at the nape of her neck. Why do I want my babies to have hair when they are born? Is it a sign of completeness, of arriving with all the things they will need in this world? To comb Cameron's thick hair is an agony for both of us. She cuts it off with her play scissors and hides her curls in a shoebox in her closet. She isn't exactly proud, and I'm not exactly pleased. The truth is, I love that she loves her freedom. I wonder how long Taylor's hair will stay white and whether he'll be happy with it—a boy who wants to learn to be rough.

My father starts to go bald and talks about how he never used to need a hat to protect the top of his head from the sun. I am told that the chemo drug Adriamycin is sure death to all my hair; at thirty-five years old, all my hair is going to fall out. I need to buy some.

I read in a beauty magazine in the doctor's office that blondes have an average of 140,000 strands of hair, brunettes 108,000, and redheads 90,000. I'm trying to get my head around this number. Is this like 140,000 pieces of uncooked spaghetti falling to the kitchen floor? My hair wants to be free, to grow, to play in the ocean just like the rest of me. I consider it a natural community leader: the one on top of the head. It wants to be a part of everything and have a social life, too.

I am told that I shouldn't worry: that it will grow back and be even curlier. People start their stories, *When my sister lost hers. . . .* But I have invested too much in my hair to listen. My hair is my home. I wore it in a French braid while I was in labor with Brooke. Some Manhattan beautician who appeared to have four hands wove it into a French twist for my friend Richard's wedding. In high school, I ironed it straight, and I twirled it with my fingers. I put blond highlights in it when it started to look dull. In the cabinet under the bathroom sink, I have dozens of curlers—hot-steamed ones, Velcro giants, and orange-juice cans. Now I am going to poison to death my prized possession. My female ensnarement. My warm hat.

I want to line up my hair like sticks of incense on my pillow. I want to get on my knees and light each bundle on fire.

Dr. Mendes tells me to send him two finger-length chunks of my hair before it falls out. He has some kind of mysterious test that can rate the amount of active cancer in the body. I try to imagine microscopic blobs floating up and down a hair shaft, neutralized by some chemical and studied for its killer properties. Should I believe it?

I have to.

My friend Robin, dressed in her favorite t-shirt that says NOWHERE TO GO BUT HERE, washes my hair for the last time before it will fall out in big clumps. Robin is also a blonde and wears her hair sculpted to her round face: short and perky. We have shared college and the birth of our children together, and now we share this. I'm afraid. The truth is: this experience is too intimate for me. The mango soap bubbles glide past my nose while Robin is chattering about her friend's husband and how he hasn't made a dime. Eyes closed, I want to relish this moment. How do I open my hair to loss? How do I help unfasten each strand from the memory that it belonged to my head? This is a specific anguish.

Robin's fingers circle, forming an arch of pressure under my neck, eulogizing my hair. I drop underwater. My ears fill and my tears flow into the soap bubbles. Long strands of hair float by my face in little whirlpools. I cry for all of us, for all women who are lying in bathtubs trying to love themselves.

In time, after the second chemo treatment, there is no hair left. I stand naked in front of the full-length mirror in my clothes closet. I am down to 105 lbs. I scan for evidence that what stands before me is a woman. Where is the female shoreline? I have no hair, no eyebrows, no eyelashes, no pubic hair, no armpit or leg hair. All I see is one little left breast, marooned.

Cameron stands next to me in the bathroom, wearing her favorite wide-brimmed straw hat. She tells me in no uncertain terms that she never wants to see me bald: *Mommy, you have to wear your scarf at home.* I tell her that my scalp itches. I think to myself that I'll buy a cotton scarf. I hope it stays on when I do the dishes, wipe my neck with wet hands, or lean over and kiss the kids goodnight.

Friends encourage me to try some wigs. I hate the look of a sculpture sitting on my head. And how do I manage my fear that, if I bend over to put on my boots, my wig will fall to the floor and look like a large Brillo pad sprawled on the white tile? What about the plastic sheen in full daylight? And how exactly do you shampoo a wig? I think of Brooke when she washes her Barbie. Her doll's hair mats until it looks like seaweed and reminds me of a ghost rising from the ocean. I watch Brooke try to brush it until it turns into a frizzy fountain of big hair.

Cameron comes home from school and tells me her friend Ashley cut off all her hair. *Two feet!* She tells me she donated it to an organization that makes wigs. I think how early in their lives our children decide they must help. Is this really their job: to make older women feel more beautiful? I wonder who is wearing Ashley and if, like this sweet girl, she has a sudden affinity for gymnastics and chocolate-filled doughnuts.

In the oncologist's waiting room I covertly check out the other bald women who are leaning over months-old *Family Circle* magazines. I play a game called Who's Wearing a Wig? The woman sitting in the corner has what I call elderly blue hair. I decide it's real. A woman around forty years old enters, wearing a sundress with bright red roses splashed all over. It looks so perky I want to puke. The woman swings herself over to the reception desk and signs in, chatting to the receptionist that she is *totally geared up* for her next chemo drip. She quickly, decisively, turns around and looks right at me looking at her. Her shoulder-length black hair comes with her in one sweeping gesture, not a hair out of place. I decide it is fake.

For eight months my scalp is smooth. I don't touch it. I am afraid of it. The top of my head belongs to someone I haven't met. It's as if I have become a warrior or a monk or a high-fashion model. I don't know these people.

I become inventive with my scarves. I'm part Bedouin, part hippie, part gypsy, part Muslim. I fold the bright geometric splashes of color over the top of my head, twist each side into cloth ropes, and then tie them at the back of my head. Friends keep bringing me new ones: orange and yellow and fuchsia; cotton and polyester and silk. I walk out of the door with daisies on my head. A father I don't know leans on his BMW in the parking lot at the kids' school. He tells me I look beautiful . . . *in that scarf*. I want to yell: *This isn't some supermodel look or something I saw on Oprah about how to dress up a bad hair day. This is chemotherapy*.

I learn to walk slowly so my scarf won't move. I see another woman in the drugstore wearing a scarf. The evidence is that she has no eyebrows. I get up the nerve to chat with her in the vitamin section. *How beautiful*, I say. *Where did you learn to wrap your scarf?* She knows that I know. She tells me she has almost finished treatment. I tell her I have four more to go. Silently, we wait in line for the cash register. I want to spill everything to her: how I avoid mirrors by changing in my closet; how violent it feels to have hot water sprayed on my naked head in the shower; how I practice dying on the beach, curled on my side and letting the wind and the sand roll me like sea grass. When we leave, we smile as if to say *Hang in there* to each other. We pull out of our parking spots at exactly the same time.

After my last chemo treatment, I go down the hill to the creek. It is late at night under a full December moon. I toss my baby-blue chenille bathrobe on the open fire in a ritual of rage. I smell the metallic burning of the drugs: Adriamycin, Methotrexate, and Cytoxan. I throw all the anti-nausea pills and the shiny green gel suppositories into the toilet. I pour the rest of the Benadryl down the sink and place the empty bottle on a little nest of Roger's brown hair in the wastebasket.

My hair grows back in white fluffy tufts. I'm like a baby bird. The kids jump onto the bed and take turns feeling my new hair. I tell them my head is a genie where any dream can come true. *Rub three times in a circle*, I say. *Then close your eyes and make any wish you want*. Taylor wants me to come to his basketball game on Friday. Cameron wishes for a new dress for her birthday. Brooke sucks her thumb and falls asleep in my lap.

There's something both exciting and strange when the thing you love the most comes back, but different. I wonder if I will outgrow these ringlets growing all over my head. My hair has never been this curly, on the verge of kinky. It's also a darker blond: the color of ash. Friends ask if they can touch it. They thread that thin line between saying nothing and too much. I can't say I don't like it. Actually, the relief of having hair makes me giddy. I roll back and forth across my pillowcase, re-joining myself to myself. I start singing when I do the laundry. My hands sweep higher when I talk, as though I have been a doll these past months, as if a few inches of protection on my head make it possible to sing Beatles songs at breakfast.

I throw out every old comb and brush I own. I find long blond hairs hanging on for their life from the plastic bristles. But I save my grandmother's brush that sits on my bureau and the matching mirror with swirls engraved on the silver handle. Her brush and mirror are noble, lined up next to each other. I want to start again. This time, I buy more expensive brushes with pale wooden handles and natural bristles: one for the car, one for the bathroom, and one for the dressing room. I will never have to throw these away. I won't grow my hair back as long as it was before. The evil witch can never climb my long tresses again.

I begin to take my hair on trips. I travel to Italy as a woman who never had cancer, whose hair happens to be short and sensual and soft. The men whistle at me on the Ponte Vecchio as I lean out over the Arno. My hair lifts in the strong breeze against a backdrop of raking Italian light. A taxi driver in Rome drives me in circles as he asks in Italian if I want to go home with him for lunch. With a huge smile, I point to my wedding ring and say *senora*. He laughs with me and says *no problemo*. I let him drop me off at my hotel and kiss my hand. He doesn't notice the fine, almost invisible white hairs on my wrist.

When I travel I find myself fascinated with other people's hair: thick, jet-black Italian hair or Scandinavian hair that is slightly brighter than the German; the traditional Quechan woman with her long black braids pulled back and tied into one; the Ugandan children who all have exactly the same hairstyle—kinked curls, two inches long, cut evenly over the bowl of their heads. I decide hair is decoration, an accessory, like jewelry or handbags.

Many years later, I travel with the kids to Belize. Taylor and Cameron have brought their fiancés and we are sitting in the waist-deep turquoise water, talking. They want to know how to create a wedding ceremony that is real. I tell them that the Japanese have a hair-combing ceremony. The bride and groom, in their separate homes, change into white silk pajamas. The bride wears new slippers. The couple prays to the ancestors while seated in front of a small table mirror. The bride faces out of the house. The groom faces in. The respective parents stroke the comb through their children's hair three times while reciting the ancient litany:

The first stroke combs to the end of life.
The second stroke brings love and respect till old age.
The third stroke brings many children.

I throw my hair back in delight when Taylor says, *Let's just go to Vegas*. I feel the movement of hair falling on me, washing me softly toward my grandchildren. The sun-trembling water catches our eyes.

I am cleaning out every desk drawer. I find old yellowed pictures of my grandmother, empty Scotch tape holders, keys to cars sold years ago. I want to bring order to my heart. I place rubber bands and paper clips to the right side of my desk drawer; passport, stamps, and a calendar of the moon phases to the left. Among a stack of bank statements I find a lock of my white hair, tied in a bow with a royal blue ribbon. I don't remember when I did this or why. I put it on the base of the lamp at my bedside. When I roll over, I face it at eye level. This lock of hair is precious and strange lying there, disconnected from my body.

The ends curl like fingertips at rest.

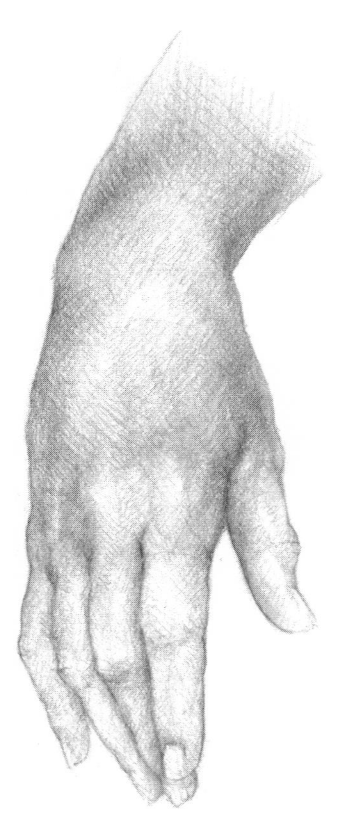

3

HAND

IT'S LIKE CLOSING YOUR EYES *and feeling with your fingers and the palm of your hand the difference between Wonder bread and whole grain*, says the pathologist. A CAT scan can only pick up a tumor two millimeters and larger. The human hand can feel the ones that are smaller. *Think about it*, he continues, *the hand is your most sensitive tool. If you smooth out a tablecloth and there's a grain of salt, you'll feel it.* First, the pathologist will slice my breast like a loaf of bread and then feel with his hands for any little seeds of cancer.

My parents expect all of us to go on an Outward Bound survival course as teenagers. They say we need to test our mettle. At sixteen, I can choose any program, no questions asked. I opt for one in the Quetico Superior Region of northern Minnesota and Canada. I love the smooth skin of any lake and the intimacy of birch trees huddled, white on white. My brother Deke trains me all summer. I run three hundred laps around the driveway in new tennis shoes and nylon red shorts while he hovers over my grandfather's stopwatch.

From the first day, our instructors prepare us for the big moment, the solo. After ten days and twenty portages we reach the lake, where we'll spend three days and nights alone with no tent, no food, and no company. I take a sleeping bag, five matches, and a fishing hook and line. My instructors, Mandy and Margo, leave me, the backs of their paddles shining wet and hopeful as they glide away. They remind me to place a rock on top of the cairn every day so they can check up on me. I'm terrified of feeling small inside the night sky and sleeping near the stands of pine trees. This is bear country.

The first evening, as I'm huddled against the darkness, a moose and her baby crash through the woods and plunge into the water. As they splash, the reddening sun lines the edge of fur on the baby's ears. I resolve not to take anything from this holy place. To my surprise, the second night they come to bathe again. The night after that, nothing.

On the fourth morning, I fall backwards into a vision. Thousands of hands start growing out of the water, each with knuckles made of little waves. Then, thousands more emerge from the rocks across the shore, each with fingers laced with lichen and moss. Yet further thousands spring from the pine trees, each palm made of branches and needles. Together, these thousands of hands climb upward, reaching into the sky to a point just above my head.

Then they clasp themselves into a solid ball. A loud thunderclap; then lightning shoots down through the top of my head.

The next thing I know, my instructors are trying to wake me up, waving smelling salts in front of my nose. The first words I utter in three days: *What is the meaning of hands?*

Years later, I have a dream:

> It's early morning and I am sitting outside at a café (maybe in Italy) drinking a cappuccino. Suddenly blood is spewing out of holes in the center of my hands, covering my white cotton skirt. I ask some man who is sitting next to me if he would grab some paper towels to plug up the holes. We use paper towel after paper towel, throwing them down with disgust.

When I wake at four a.m. the house is quiet. I turn on the bedside lamp and check my hands. In the center of each palm is a small, but real lump. I can't straighten my fingers. I search my palms for a divine message. I read that physicians over the centuries have not succeeded in curing these stigmata wounds. Sometimes the wounds mist a floral perfume.

According to Antoine Imbert-Gourbeyre in *La Stigmatisation*, "The life of a stigmatic is a long series of sorrows which arise from the Divine malady of the stigmata and end only in death." By the end of the nineteenth century, which was when his book was published, he estimated that there'd been 321 stigmatics, beginning with St. Francis of Assisi, whose ranks I appear to have joined. I'll take this dream elevation—especially this morning, as the kids whine over the lunch choices. I'll take the bright blood and even the breast cancer. But I'm not thrilled by "a long series of sorrows ending in death." My palms, with their little bumps, leak.

On the dock in Canada, I sit with my father talking about the clouds overhead. We watch Titan, his black Labrador, swimming in circles. Dad tells me he is to have another surgery, and he shows me his hands, how he can't flatten his palms against the armrest of his chair. He has Dupuytren's contracture. He tells me it's more common in people with Irish, Scottish, and Scandinavian backgrounds. *What next?* he laughs. Carefully, I examine his hands, turning them from one side to the other. Sure enough, he has a nodule in the center of each palm. I think he must be a stigmatic, too.

My father used to call hands *the finest tools on earth*. Dr. Thompson's hands are precise and serene in the way they slide and latch over the metal edge of the machine. *We want to check the pressure against your eardrum*, he says. His hands are close to my cheek. I notice two thick veins running parallel and then diving into the fold of his wrist. I need to count on this surgeon's hands, because in two days they will drill a hole the size of a half-dollar into the back of my skull, behind my right ear, and approach my inner ear through, as he says, *the back door*. He explains that the inner ear is like a room within a room within a room. Dr. Thompson will then place a tiny valve into the inner ear chamber to regulate the fluid.

The doctor holds up the device that he invented. His hands, backlit, are a burgundy color, as though all the blood in his body is collecting itself to pinch the tube between his thumb and index finger. Everything is precise. I smell the disinfectant on his wrists. He tells me the procedure will take about five or six hours. As he leaves the room he reassures me he will be very careful not to nick my facial nerve.

The first thing I see when I wake from surgery is a hand hovering, like a hummingbird, to my right and flapping this way and that. *I'm checking the bandages*, Dr. Thompson says. *They're not quite tight enough*. He pats my left shoulder. *You did very well. It took longer than we thought; your inner ear is so small and protected.*

I try to respond but my voice is floating through the anesthesia, the morning fog thick and viscous. *Thank you for your careful hands*, I want to say. *Thank you for helping me stand.*

A year later I call Dr. Thompson's office to schedule a checkup. The receptionist tells me that he's no longer working as a surgeon, but is teaching instead. He had an accident. *He loves to scuba dive*, she says, *and he came up too fast and got the bends.* She pauses. *He lost the use of his hands.*

I stay through the night with Robin, the day before the doctors take her little boy, my godson Justin, off the respirator. They will remove his ten-year-old eyes and kidneys and put them in the body of a sixty-year-old. Robin's hands move across the surface of Justin's body under the white sheet—a body swollen and bruised from the accident where a car ran into him. Robin's hands look miraculously buoyant, like ships floating just above the waterline. She tells me she is memorizing her son's body: the way his hip bones lift, the smooth skin behind his knees. I sit next to her, leaning over the rail of the hospital bed. I pass my hand over hers, my palm weeping. We shed tears for a boy who loves the Broncos, who dresses up as his own tombstone on Halloween, who looks like Dennis the Menace. My hands follow Robin's toward Justin's head and they cup themselves under the back of his neck. They remember.

On the morning of Justin's birth, there was a sudden snowstorm and Robin opened quickly. The midwives didn't make it in time and I heard Robin yelling on the toilet. She wanted to push and my heart was pounding. I laid her down on a sheet on the floor and told her, *I can do this*. Justin's head was crowning and his wet blond hair fell on my hands and the cord wrapped twice around his neck. I told Robin's husband to cut the cord with scissors and Robin to *push hard* to get Justin out. He slid into my hands.

Now the same hands hold his head. His eyes are closed forever. My fingertips want to push him back into the warm water of Robin's body, now hunched over the railing by his hospital bed, her hands pleading.

Her right baby finger is flecked with blood.

For two years, I avoid taking another medical test. But my oncologist wants to have a baseline picture of my pancreas, because both of my father's parents died of pancreatic cancer. *We want to protect you at all costs*, he says. Daryl, the MRI technician, puts a black plastic bulb into my right hand and then pulls the switch that slides me into the metal cylindrical cave. He tells me to squeeze the bulb if I feel panicked. My feet are sucked down the tunnel, and my heart starts sliding. *Don't move an inch,* Daryl says. But I can move my precious hand. I can squeeze the buoy floating in my right palm, bobbing on this cold river of death. Daryl speaks to me through a microphone. His voice is suspended over my belly.

Hold your breath for fifteen counts. One . . . two . . . three . . . four. . . . I can't decide if I should panic.

The male hand, the power grip.

The female hand, the precision grip.

The male hand, good for holding heavy weapons.

The female hand, good for making lace.

I remember watching Sarah, her high cheekbones and narrow chin pointing down to the beads in her lap. Sarah, a refugee from the civil war in northern Uganda and HIV positive, is rolling beads out of brightly colored magazine paper. She has precision hands. Her African fingertips dance, black and pink, like a flamingo in flight. She shows me her technique. My paper, listing to the side, makes a bulbous bead with a point; my earnestness is her joy. Laughter floats out of her mouth; her fingers rest on mine, shaping and lifting. I like to believe that our fingers together might signal the end of poverty. I'd like to believe that our hope might be this precision.

My wedding ring has gone, and a ghost circles its place on the second finger of my left hand.

The day Roger and I buy it, San Francisco Bay is crowned in light. Tiffany's, I'm told, means Romance, with a capital R; truthfully, it takes only five minutes to choose. I love the way the ring shines—understated, sophisticated, and petite—as it rests in the case on a black velvet throne behind the two-carat solitaires, proud and platinum. It's a yellow-gold band of baby diamond chips, alternating with midnight-blue sapphires, wrapped around each other like jewel-coiled snakes. The saleslady has a classy nametag with some shiny stone glued on the lower left. She flits around the cases, showing me other possibilities. She suggests *something more dramatic. Your fingers are so long and elegant they can handle more sparkle*. My mother used to call these kinds of fingers *candle wands*. I smile inside her compliment but don't try another one on that finger.

The Romans called the ring finger the *digitus medicus*, the medical digit. They believed a nerve runs from the ring finger to the heart. On December 17th, 1976, Roger takes the ring out of his navy blue jacket pocket and slides it on my finger. For twenty-five years it remains there. I don't take it off even to clean it or when one of the little sapphires chips. I talk the nurse into letting me leave it on during my mastectomy surgery. *Moral support*, I plead.

Thirty years later, I hold out my left hand and stare at its bareness. I am naked in bed. The cuticle of my index finger needs cutting. I'm searching to see if I have that phantom feeling, like the presence of my absent breast moving with me when I roll over. All that remains, however, is a slight indentation on the front side of my finger. My marriage is a compression of flesh. I still cannot believe it.

. . .

A June night in Marrakech. I smell the oily aroma of lamb shanks cooking, and watch the thick smoke drift in whirlpools around the bare lightbulbs that hang above us. Cameron and I are in Morocco for an adventure and to celebrate her graduation from college. We wander the medina, flow by Berber music and vegetable stalls and men who ogle at us. A gypsy woman with long gray hair tangled in a black cotton scarf and draped in a purple velvet dress squats on the ground in front of a low-lying table. Dozens of people are huddled around, watching her rough, wrinkled hands move the Tarot cards. The gypsy catches my eyes and holds them for a moment in the smoky air. Our translator, Mohammed, tells me that this woman is famous in Marrakech and that she's been working in the medina for thirty years. *Her prophesies are never wrong*, he adds.

We push in further. The gypsy woman grabs my hand and pulls me toward her. Mohammed says she wants to read my palms. She never looks me in the eyes again. She traces the lifeline deeply set across my palm. *Do you see these side lines?* she asks me through Mohammed. *These are the lines of war. Strange for a woman*. Her finger stops at an intersection under the pad of my baby finger. One large and two smaller lines cross the lifeline. *Three children*, she continues. *The loves of your life. But see the large white line here? You are mother to the whole world.*

As we leave, I lean into the hot, dense night as though it were solid. I look down at my hands, still warm from the gypsy's touch, and scan for the signs of love and war.

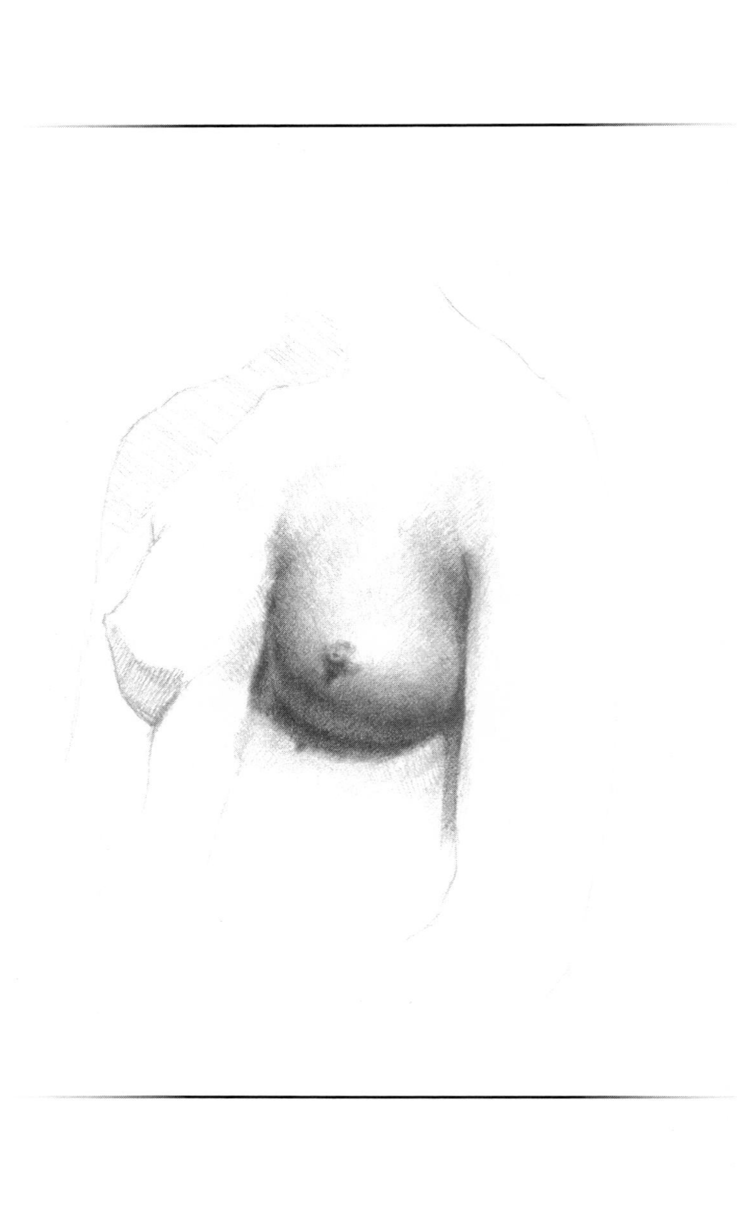

4

The Left Breast

THE LETTER from Boulder Community Hospital spells my name wrong. *Dear Jenny*, it begins. *Your mammogram is inconclusive. A magnification is necessary. Please call and schedule your appointment.* I am collecting words like *magnification* and *inconclusive*. Their definitions have their own kind of severity: *magnification*—to enlarge; *inconclusive*—to not put an end to doubt. They have their own kind of honesty, too. To magnify the truth: life is inconclusive.

The letter is inconvenient. A week after its arrival, I am due to fly back to Uganda to join the women who are raising themselves out of poverty through BeadforLife, the women's project that Torkin and Devin and I had started the previous year, and of which Sarah is a part. I originally took Brooke and Cameron to Uganda to join Torkin and her husband to work with HIV-positive women, as well as to volunteer in various orphanages. We saw women in a refugee camp on the outskirts of Kampala rolling beautiful jewelry out of colorful recycled paper. When we returned to the U.S., we decided to start a project selling their bracelets and necklaces.

This time, I will enter their huts and sit on the dusty ground. We will chat about their new babies and the new chair in the corner. The bright paper beads they sell will hang from the ceiling in long, shiny strands. Then I'll leave though the beaded-curtain doorway and watch how these women's long hands grip the yellow plastic jerry cans high on their heads. I'll notice their lime, orange, and blue dresses hanging on the line to dry, along with the fuchsia and purple scarves, the color of Ugandan flowers, which the women wind three times around their heads. But before I leave for Kampala, I am to be magnified and examined for conclusions.

I arrive at the hospital and am given a green cotton shift to wear—a shade of green that resembles nothing alive. I open the shift in front of an x-ray machine that swings, then presses and flashes a light so dangerous the technician leaps and hides behind a lead shield. This is not the African sun. I slide in my wool socks on a nondescript, sterilized floor and not on dry soil. The technician and I both smile—professionally, politely, our teeth hidden. *You can dress now*, she says.

I feel like an obedient child as I follow the exit signs leading out of the Women's Center into the main part of the hospital. It is as if I'm following the bread crumbs that take me out of the dark woods. The afternoon light is bright, shining off the sea of cars in the parking lot. I notice a few ash trees forced to grow between rows of cement.

When I arrive at Entebbe, the airport is quiet. It is five thirty a.m. The air is sweet and humid. Huge gray-and-white and lemon-yellow birds lift out of the Matoke trees. My Ugandan friend Ezra tells me about his family and the size of the rain they had the other night. His gentleness means everything to me. That afternoon in the refugee camp, the women come running: *Way bale nyo*, they shout in greeting. The widest smile in a year spreads across my face. Margaret points to her new baby boy on the hip of one of her daughters, who isn't more than six years old. Dozens of children in torn t-shirts and shorts are playing with sticks and orange peels. The refugee camp is flapping with chatter and hung laundry and children giggling. Everything is music. In Africa, I don't have to think: about mammograms, the new curtains in my bedroom, the sky above my house.

When I arrive back in the United States, I receive another letter. *Dear Jenny*, it begins (again). *Please call to schedule a needle biopsy*.

Dr. Bennett asks me to lie facedown on the table. My left breast hangs through a hole in the table—isolating beauty. The rest of my body disappears. Dr. Bennett keeps walking back to the x-ray films, then back to my breast. He marks spots on my breast with a black ink pen. There are so many little calcifications. It's like a field of stars, I think; my breast, a self-contained night full of starlight. I push my breast down farther. I show Dr. Bennett a larger sky to search; I want him to find what he is looking for. As gently as possible, Dr. Bennett sticks eight needles in and pulls out as many stars as he can.

The results are sent over to my oncologist, with whom after seventeen years I am on a first-name basis. Mark. A new photo of the fine woodworked walnut table he just finished making is on the wall. His wife is still recovering from her car accident. Mark never hides behind my file. He simply places it on his desk carefully and wheels his chair closer. He takes my left hand.

You have breast cancer again.

My shoulders drop into the bed of my body. I begin to cry what I call *female tears*, like a low mist over a river. This time, however, I feel no shock. My children and Roger are not with me. This is my own room. I know its length and width: the simple, spare, metal furniture; the black-and-silver blood-pressure cuff hanging on the wall next to the door; the crisp roll of paper on the examining table; the antibacterial liquid soap above the sink.

I have Carcinoma in Situ (CIS), which means the cancer has stayed in its place, behaving itself. For now. Mark explains that the cancer can stay in the duct for years and that there's no way of knowing when it might break out. My breast has become a landscape of underground pipes that can explode at any time.

At home, I practice mouthing the words in front of the mirror: *Take my breast.* I want to be done. Years of vigilance have made my fingers cautious as they roam over my body: a thick spot near my nipple, a strange bump on my big toe, three days of unexplained exhaustion. My body has become a road map of hairpin turns. I never know what's down the ravine and if my fingers will get caught in a tangle of cells gone wild.

I want to tell my body that it's safe now, that there's no tissue remaining that can turn on it. But I choose not to include the 5 percent of tissue that Mark tells me the surgeon won't be able to cut out. I want to say, *It's time to sleep*. I wander around the kitchen, cleaning surfaces, once again trying to comprehend how the body begins with two of everything, in case a body part fails or we lose one. This is the body's math: two minus one equals one; one minus one equals none.

I move down the list, my imaginary pencil filling in the circles under family history:

Heart disease: *no*

Diabetes: *yes* (Explain: *paternal grandfather*)

Liver disease: *no*

History of depression: *no*

Cancer: *yes* (Explain: *maternal grandmother, maternal grandfather, paternal grandfather, paternal grandmother, maternal aunt, paternal uncles [2], mother, and father*)

Colon cancer: *no*

Brain cancer: *no*

Bone cancer: *no*

Pancreatic cancer: (Explain: *paternal grandmother, paternal grandfather*)

Melanoma: *no*

Lymphoma: *yes* (Explain: *maternal grandfather*)

Breast cancer: *yes* (Explain: *maternal grandmother, mother, aunt*)

If this applies to you
Surgeries: *mastectomy, 1990, right side*.

Ten years after I lose my first breast my mother calls. *Guess what, Gin*, she says, *me too*. Her voice sounds strangely exasperated as though the day had been enough without this. She tells me the cancer cells are contained in the ducts, just like her own mother's breast cancer.

She keeps her breast.

That same year, my brother Deke is limping. I watch him walk down the dock leaning on a stick. He calls the surgeon to schedule a hip replacement. *Seems to run in the family*, he says. *We hit fifty, and we need a mechanic*. I ask him when he's thinking of having the surgery. *Sometime at the end of the duck season*, he says. *So I can hopefully ski in the spring*. He gets to replace it.

In nine days, I will lose my other breast. I'm happy to be at the beach this week. It's easier to be naked, to watch my body unfold in the warm waters of the Caribbean, for the mother waters to hold me. I raise my breast to the surface. The water doesn't praise my breast or me, or make anything too precious of either of us. She simply rolls me over and opens my arms. Above me, I see the white wings of a seagull.

There will be no more mammograms, no more sitting in the Women's Center staring at other women reading magazines in pale-blue cotton robes, Velcroed at the front. No more wipe-it swipes for my armpits; no more asking the technician about whether it is harder to squish a big breast or a tiny one; no more little sticky tags marking old biopsies. No more holding my breath when they shoot the picture; no more nurses ducking behind the plastic screen that looks like a motorcycle windshield; no more reminder letters from Boulder Community Hospital with the green logo of the Rocky Mountains.

I cup my left breast under the covers, checking to feel it is there. I still need it attached. My grandmother's eighty-year-old best friend, who grew up on a farm, once told me that she thought her old-lady breasts looked like burlap bags with lumpy potatoes inside. Another of her friends says hers look like little hoses. I grew up near a small town: my breast looks like a peach with the stem still attached, not ready for picking.

Cameron flies out from San Francisco to be with me for the surgery. At twenty-six, she comes home to do what she couldn't do at seven. She wants to turn into the storm. Her wisdom makes me weep.

The night before—May 29th, 2007, the same week, and seventeen years after the first breast—I ask Roger to join me with the kids to sit in the cave I have dug in the hillside down by the creek. I made it following a dream I had that all women need a place to go underground. I light a fire in the clay-domed fireplace and spread out wool blankets and wait at the entrance for them. Taylor and his girlfriend Nicole walk down the hill holding hands, light and unconcerned. I love the way they occupy each other. Cameron and Brooke follow like twins, their long strides navigating the boulders in unison. They are wearing sandals and jeans, their hair pulled back in ponytails, chatting. Roger walks ponderously with Tai, our melancholic Australian shepherd. He scans the ground for thistles to pull out with his bare hands.

When they each stoop under the thick ledge of the stone roof, the fire brightens their faces. My family sit huddled with their arms wrapped around their knees in the tight womb. They are everything I love—a love that's contained in the details: Brooke's beige baseball hat; the black Egyptian kohl lining Nicole's eyes; Cameron's blue-green sweater with the black stripe on the sleeve; Taylor's glance around the cave; Roger's impossibly huge feet. To ease everyone's anxiety I tell them somberly that we are going to have a five-hour New Age ceremony. We find our way to laughter.

I tell them, *I don't want this night to go unnoticed. Last time, you were too young for your dad and I to use words like mastectomy and death. We simply told you the doctors needed to make a cut and that I would be in the hospital for a few days and that you could visit. Then we tucked you in bed. This is a different story. I am not as afraid. I am not terrified of losing you. I'm just sad. I never wanted to lose so much.*

Cameron begins to cry, deeply. She remembers how scared she felt. She tells us that she used to go to bed, her legs pulled up to her chest, holding her stuffed bear. This time she wants to spend the night in the hospital bed, holding me. Brooke cries when Cameron does. She remembers her feelings of terror the afternoon her father brought her to the hospital and she saw the IV tube coming out of my arm. She thought I would have that in my arm forever. She tells us this time she's not sure she will be able to look at it. I tell her I will put a towel over it.

Taylor looks down at his feet. He speaks slowly of how he doesn't remember much of the last time and how badly he feels that he doesn't. Finally, he says softly, *I can't stand that you have to go through more*. He wants it over. Roger is listening, silent. He says there isn't anything left to say.

The next day, the nurse offers me a tranquilizer. The anesthesiologist stands by my bedside and shakes my hand. I look into his eyes with a dreamy smile. I suspect he has worn horn-rimmed glasses since he was a little boy. I am checking to see how I feel about putting my life in his hands. I notice the nail on his right index finger is broken; the thick veins in his hands are raised, and his gold wedding ring is rubbed soft. The white string at the back of his gown is hanging over his shoulder, and his throaty voice hides a melody. His square, balanced football shoulders make me think he's a Bronco fan.

I want to tell him to treat me as if I was his own daughter.

When I wake up I feel a rhythmic pressure squeezing my legs. The nurse explains that the pumping leg-wraps prevent blood clots after surgery. They are driving me crazy. At midnight, Cameron and I furtively glance at the door and conduct a covert mission to peel them off. My legs are finally free and we laugh together like naughty children. Cameron sits on my bed and tells me that I woke up out of the anesthesia crying. She says I tapped my chest as though I was trying to reassure myself that I was still a woman. Cameron tells me that I am beautiful and tucks the blanket over my chest. My hand reaches under my gown and presses the bandages.

It's gone, my daughter tells me gently. *It's gone*.

. . .

I am learning the meaning of *recovery*. It is more than a return to a normal condition. It is the act of regaining or saving something lost.

A praying mantis walks across my bed covers—a tiny green sleeve, a shining scrim of legs. I decide it is making its way home. Lying in bed for days, I watch each evening the purple and red glow of sunset. I think how everything returns to its place. *In what home*, I wonder, *is my amputated breast sleeping?*

My friends tell me they are sorry I have been in bed so long. Meanwhile, deep-pink clouds line the horizon; their thin bodies form, then dissolve.

I'm not sorry for my body. But my soul hasn't walked the crackling fields next door for many days, and I miss them. A kingfisher flicks by my bedroom window and I lie and marvel at him: how finely the feathers are tufted on his head, how he lands so precisely on the lower branch of the cottonwood.

I look from my belly button downward. My tummy is flat. I glance up to my eyes in the glass reflection of the cabin. They are watchful, waiting for a nod perhaps, or a wink—some sign of approval or confirmation that my arms, legs, pelvis, and chest are still mine. The left side of my chest feels tight, foreign. It's not soft or open like the right and I can't remember how many years it took for me to feel that this was now my body. A doctor friend explains that the sensation I now have on the left side of my chest is because the sensory cortex carries a rough map of the body, which is called a *homunculus* or, affectionately, the *little man*. He says that each body part in the homunculus is wired to its corresponding portion of the real anatomy. When you have a mastectomy, the homunculus rewires its circuitry to make up for the signals it was no longer receiving from the chest wall. He takes my hand: *This is why you have a phantom breast that sometimes can feel sensation*. I find dread in the back of my knees. I say to myself, *OK little woman, you can handle this loss*.

I try to navigate the passage of going from two to one to none.

I dream:

> I am crossing a channel of water in a car. The water is up to the seats. My friend Robert is driving and I tell him that this has happened before; we will be OK. The force of the current on each side is powerful. But I know there is a straight shot through.

I have to fit myself into a new, tighter body, one that's been peeled like a birch tree where all the ant channels are exposed. It is a birch with no bark, and no leaves where my breasts were. I have to find a way to make my chest the sunlight that feeds the tree.

My friends convince me that I should go to a plastic surgeon, to check out the options. As befitting his work, Dr. Scott's office is thoroughly plastic. It has orange chairs and a dirty-white coffee table displaying photo albums of "new" breasts. Perched behind her plastic sliding window, the receptionist asks for my insurance card. I explain that I am here for a free consultation. She shrugs and withdraws into her booth. I slink into the 1960s plastic chair and reach for the album with the plastic sleeve and the handwritten label on the lower-right corner, "Trans Flap Breast Reconstruction," and read about how one takes one part of the body to build a new part. It sounds like stealing.

The first photos are of women with their shirts pulled up, revealing a nasty, thick scar that runs across the panty line from hip to hip. The text explains that they pull a portion of skin, fat, and muscle from the lower abdomen and slide it up to the breast area to build a new one. We are adding new scars. But, the text continues, *You get a tummy tuck while you are at it.* (Is this what it means to receive a booby prize?) I notice that not one of the six women showing their bellies has a smile on her face.

Midway through the album we get to the breasts themselves. I sink lower down in my chair. I am scanning for something that looks natural, slightly misshapen, or surrendered to gravity, perhaps a mole near the armpit. They are showing me mounds of flesh that look like Renaissance-sculptured breasts stuck on the body. They have no transparency, no shafts of light passing through the flesh; they do not seem beautiful to touch. I am grief-stricken for all of us. I don't even want to know the names of these women. Toward the back of the album I get to the section called "Nipple and Areola Reconstruction." At once fascinated and horrified, I read:

> There are generally three areas from which nipple grafts are commonly harvested. These include: the opposite nipple, the

labia, and the earlobe. In general, the opposite nipple provides the best color and texture match for the missing nipple.

In patients with a large nipple on the opposite breast, some of this nipple may be used to reconstruct the missing nipple. The remaining nipple is divided and the distal portion is used. The graft of the nipple may be bisected, with one half being used for the missing nipple. The remaining half of the nipple is then simply repaired by direct suture closure. However, in patients who have had bilateral mastectomies, this is not a possibility as there is no remaining nipple to use.

The labia and earlobe provide alternative donor sites. A triangular wedge is removed from either the labia or the earlobe and it is grafted to the appropriate position on the reconstructed breast. One drawback with this type of nipple reconstruction is that the bulk and projection can be less than optimal. The defect in the labia or earlobe is simply closed directly. These types of nipple reconstructions are particularly useful in patients who have had bilateral reconstructions, as the option of using the patient's own nipple is not available.

I arrange the album on the table next to the ones with titles like "Chin and Throat Reconstruction," "Face Lifts," and "Liposuction." I look down, examining the mud stain on my right black boot. *Damn the dirt driveway in the winter*, I think. The nurse calls my name twice before I lift my head. I follow her into the examining room where she points to another orange plastic chair for me to sit in. I convince myself that this is a good idea.

At least it's good to know what you are not choosing, people say. I wish I'd seen magic in those pictures—a picture of a heron flying low over the morning haze; a young woman, bare-breasted, leaping in the field.

Instead, I find myself thumbing through an album of tattoo designs at the Enchanted Ink in downtown Boulder. I've no idea what has gotten into me. I always thought tattoos were for biker guys or military men or drug addicts. Besides, I am too old for this. But I see beauty in these roses and hearts and doves.

I ask for the woman tattooist, Elaine. I tell her how I admire those women who have flowering vines or intricate flowers trailing over their chest scars. Elaine tells me that the most painful area would be exactly where I want to put it. I'm not ready for more pain. I decide to hide the tattoo on my butt, only to be discovered by intimates or as my signature, like when they identify the body in murder shows by the mole on the rear right cheek. I want to say, *If you're going to take parts of my body, I'm going to replace them with a thing of beauty*. I decide on a tiger lily, which is an elegant yellow lily with six petals and three green leaves and a tiger's face in the center. It feels completely right, an expression of fierce beauty. Elaine brings out the small palette of black, yellow, and green paint and her needle gun. I don't feel the pain; the needle feels like a cat scratching for new life.

I have afternoon tea with Ana, a friend of a friend. She wears a long skirt in three tiers, each a riot of color and pattern that has nothing to do with the next layer. Her sheer cream blouse is romantic with flouncy sleeves. She's studying women's ritual and mythology and wants to interview me on my cancer experience and any rituals I use in my healing.

What rituals do you use to get through this? she asks. I tell her of three:

- I always get out of bed and make breakfast for the kids.
- I sit on the bathroom floor after a shower and rub almond oil over every part of my body.
- I look everyone in the eyes.

She tells me I am like the Sumerian goddess Inanna going through the seven gates of the underworld, stripped of something precious at each threshold until she arrives at the center of the earth, utterly naked. Inanna is hung on a meat hook. *But don't worry*, says Ana, *she gets saved by her sister and brought back to the upper world.* As we finish the interview, I want to give Ana a lecture on the failure of imagination, on the chasm between skin and story. How many millions of women are left hanging and burnt on stakes and have no sisters to rescue them?

I read in the *Chicago Tribune* that crews with backhoes and bulldozers have demolished the Pennsylvania schoolhouse where ten Amish girls were gunned down. The site will be seeded and left as pasture. I reflect on this idea of destroying to heal, to bring down the house so new grass can grow. I think of the Amish mothers picking wildflowers on the site in later years, the blooms of their dead daughters.

My breasts have gone to seed.

. . .

A new therapy client tells me that she's recently been diagnosed with breast cancer. Her name is Nancy and she is forty-two years old and beautiful, with pale skin and thick, luscious lips. We instantly like each other. She feels like a little sister. My heart grips when it comes to the age of her children, nine and twelve. She says that her husband doesn't want to touch her—*there*—as though a part of her body is roped off.

I tell her the landscape of her condition is rugged. *At times, it's so steep you'll feel like you can't breathe*, I continue. *But there will be beautiful meadows along the way. You will stop and lay down on the earth and give all your sorrow away. You will cry and feel like you can't go on. Then you will get up and go to the grocery store and buy fresh peaches and cream for dessert. You will cut them in perfect slices and lay them in four bowls and pour cream over their juicy flesh. You will offer them to your family as the sweetest thing you have ever known. The order of what really matters will find you.*

These days will come like presents.

Nancy leaves with confidence in her spine, as though her backbone is aligned with all women who walk the same terrain. I realize that I am far away from this place, on a new road, one that has nothing to do with impossible choices like steering left toward lumpectomy and radiation or right toward mastectomy; or left toward Tamoxifen or right toward oopherectomy.

There are simple crossroads: Shall it be eggs for breakfast or oatmeal?

Instead, I drive on and on, occasionally stopping to look over the plains toward the back mountain range. My body is finally balanced. I have no breasts. I am no longer leaning toward one, no longer slipping out of my skin, fleeing for the five-thousand-foot view. This is it: a chest wall, with symmetry; two perfect quartz veins running horizontally. They do not touch each other. They outline a new continent, a clear cut. That chest wall is one I will scale every day with my own hand.

But I will always miss my first landscape.

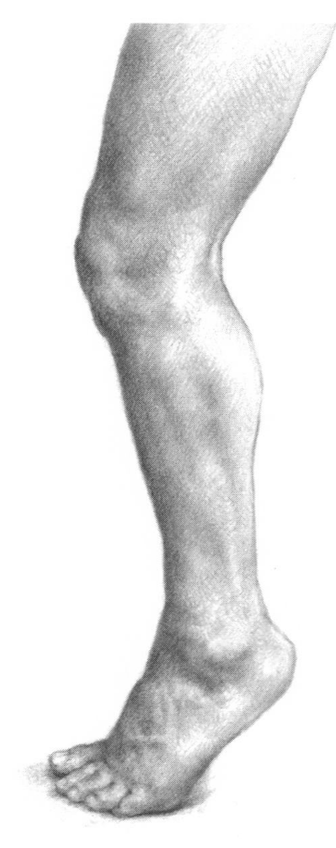

5

LEG

I AM EIGHT YEARS OLD when I find a pair of my brother's old crutches in the basement. I practice walking around in the cool darkness. I trapeze around the boxes of children's books and the stacks of every imaginable piece of athletic equipment. I feel lighter and lighter, swinging this way and that, as if my imagined injury would give me a place in this family of men, as if I'm tougher than wood. I want a pretend broken leg in order to belong. I fake such intense pain that no one wants to touch it. I convince them my leg's not broken by rotating my ankle in circles. My seasoned mother says, *Sprains are always more painful than breaks*.

I love the smell of the Ace bandages and the little clips that keep the elastic from unraveling. I keep the secret of my fake leg for an entire week. I am wheeled around school, receiving help to climb the stairs of the bus. I gather sympathy like roses. I like how my toes look, slender shoots poking out of the bandages—like something vulnerable and newborn.

When I am "healed," I chase my father's long legs around the living room, trying not to kick the tinted-amber glass doors of the gun case. The soft wood butts of his rifles rest in red velvet cradles: upright, like tall soldiers. On a cold, clear October morning I go to the marsh with him. I am ten years old and excited beyond words to be included in this private, male ritual of hunting, this grave and beautiful run toward death. My father instructs me: *Walk like an Indian. We don't want to scare the ducks away*. I slink lower in my brother's ripped black-rubber boots. I try hard to lift my legs from my thighs so my boots won't make a squishy sound in the wide holes of mud, filled with early morning rain.

We sit in the blind, a structure built of mud and sticks wrapped in khaki-green and dark-brown camouflage. It's just like a bunker in the movies, where soldiers hide. Sach, our golden retriever (*the best one yet*, my father says), sends a plume of smoke from his panting tongue into the thin blue air. My father extends his legs out in front of him. His boots are still caked with mud from his last shoot. I copy him and stretch out my legs next to his. My left foot touches his knee. He places his index finger on his lips—*shhhh*—while I rustle in my down parka pocket for a piece of Juicy Fruit gum.

Shhhh. They're coming.

Suddenly, there's an explosion of wings rising over the hill. Before I know it, we're standing. A beautiful dark string of birds stretches and lengthens like a piece of elastic before us. My father takes my hand and squeezes—just before he raises his gun, the silver firing-pin shining; just before he squeezes the trigger and becomes a killer.

Bang. And then another. *Bang*. The second-to-last duck in line buckles. His body pitches gracefully, lifting up for a moment, then falling, beak first, as if twirling in a ballet. The bird takes a long time to come to ground—long enough for me to count three 360-degree turns. Meanwhile, Sach is racing across the edge of the marsh, my father behind him, and me behind my father. Adrenaline pumps through my hands. Then there is the shock of the bloody, wet carcass, the neck twisted around a stand of twigs. My father takes hold of the duck's beak with his glove and we walk back in silence, my two steps to his one, the duck swinging like a rag in his hand. I wipe my eyes. I don't want my father to see the size of my tears.

Years later, my four brothers carry my father up the steep, rocky path to the main cabin on Cricket Island. His bad leg drapes over my brother Jeff's arm like something that was severed and poorly reattached. When my brothers gently drop my father into the Adirondack chair on the porch, he thrusts his arms upward with his palms facing outward, and smiles. It is his signature "raise the roof" gesture. We laugh, uncomfortably, not knowing what to do with the awkwardness of a seventy-five-year-old man being carried by his own children up the path of his childhood. His bad leg rests on a birch-bark stool: his granddaughter hops over it; his dog limbos under it. I sit on the coffee table next to it. His leg becomes the center of every conversation.

I wonder what would have happened if my father had listened to the doctors twenty-five years earlier when he was diagnosed with cancer. They wanted to cut off his leg from the hip down, *to get it all*, as the doctors said. My father tells me with a big shit-eating grin that he held on to his leg because it would have been impossible to wade into a stream and fish in a wheelchair. But, he said, he could lean on his canes and throw a fly rod. He used to practice his technique in the backyard, trying to hit the old swimming pool choked under thorns and dead grape leaves. I would hear him whoop when the fly landed in the water.

He tells me that his legs still want to feel the earth, whether scuttling over the raw hillsides that sink into trout streams in Idaho, or striding across the Argentine Pampas. I know he means mischief—like he did when he crawled into the woods with all the kids on Cotsworth Island on the lake to set up traps for the bear with the blue never-sink—this bear that never existed but surely stopped our hearts. Or when he snuck tiptoe into the pantry after dinner for a tablespoon of Hershey's Syrup.

I remember his leg before cancer and the way he walked. He would meander, then pause, as though there might be a mockingbird in the elm tree. *Right over there*, he'd say. And then he'd pick up again as if there might be something else *over there*. But now there is no more bending to pick up our fallen socks or dancing hulas with friends; no more giant tennis serves or late-night kitchen raids.

A year and a half before he dies, my father breaks his bad leg. The doctor says that it was inevitable. Dad had driven the golf cart early in the morning when the sprinklers whirl around, watering the greens. Titan, his black lab, ran alongside. When he cruised back into the garage, his leg swung out and hit the side of the building. His leg hung over the side of the cart, strangely on its own.

Now my father's foot hangs off the edge of the metal hospital bed. I notice his long toes, famous in the family for gripping cherry tomatoes off the vine in my mother's garden. The nurse scrapes at the six-inch, open wound along his shinbone—a wound that went undetected for a month beneath the plaster cast. She tells me she has to rub hard enough to draw fresh blood.

Healing is never what you think, she says.

I hold my father's hand. *Hi Dad*, I whisper. His eyes stray inside their silence. A milky screen wraps his retinas like a lunar eclipse. His mind is slipping. He is trying to find me in the cool space between our hands as I unfasten my palms from his and stroke his forehead. The nurse continues to wrap the wound with long sheets of cotton.

I remember his leg—its stride, its generosity, how it always found those who were left behind and then strapped them to the thigh above it to carry them to higher ground. It was a leg that built futures and gave assistance to anyone who was sincere. It could dance with little girls at weddings and run down the football field with sons. It had helped set up tents in Alaska and had lain down by the stream's edge to feel the rush of cold water. It ached when the air pressure changed.

My mom and I always talk about our legs. *Damn heredity*, she says, as she checks her ankles for puffiness before we board any plane. Her mother suffered from gout, and now her daughter and granddaughter all hold water in their legs. It is our female lineage, as if the ocean got trapped there, sloshing around, making our legs ache. We agree our legs aren't so pretty in skirts, but my mother nonetheless wears them to meetings. I tell her she looks great and I mean it; she's a woman who goes out into the world as a woman. *Fluid retention is one of the signs of Ménière's disease,* my doctor says. Bad legs are connected to bad ears.

The night before I call the dermatologist, I dream that a huge black evil bug from outer space flies like a time-lapse, fast-moving cloud scene and lands on a very specific spot on my right upper thigh. When I wake up and roll over and look where it "landed," I discover a tiny dark mole that I never noticed before. When I ask for the next available appointment, I am told it will be in three months.

I know it's bad, I insist.

With an audible sigh, the nurse squeezes me in on Friday, before Dr. Housden's regular patients. The doctor looks at my leg.

I came in early for this? he squawks.

I convince him to remove the mole anyway. Three days later, the doctor himself calls and tells me he has egg on his face. Three separate labs have confirmed what he didn't believe: my little tiny mole is the stage before melanoma. He tells me that I have to come in and have a deeper, wider cut on my leg.

We gotta get the margins, he says. *Call in the troops.*

This is army talk—the language of invasion and defense.

. . .

My Quechuan friend Julia, an expert in plant medicines, takes me on rounds as she treks in the Peruvian Andes to check up on her patients. The first woman we visit emerges from her hut when Julia whistles, and greets us with a toothless smile. She is so excited to see us that her hands flap in random circles like a bird trying to make up its mind where to land. Breathless, the woman points to the door and we duck under the soft alpaca blanket into the dark room.

A young boy runs out with a fistful of coins to buy the beer. I notice the old man sitting on a woven mat in the corner. The smoke from the fire makes his eyes look detached and floating, as though he's a goblin sitting beneath the cast-iron pot that hangs from the thatched ceiling. His name is Carlos, and he wears a white Calvin Klein t-shirt ripped at the shoulder. His black cotton trousers are rolled up to his thighs. He has no legs. The right stump is bandaged with newspaper and twine. Julia opens jars of salves and begins to unwrap the newspaper, filthy with old blood and caked dirt. Carlos, meanwhile, looks straight ahead.

I kneel and take Carlos's hand. Through the thick clouds of smoke, I find his eyes, dark gray, like flint. Julia tells me he has sat on this dirt floor for twenty years. His children circle around him as though he is a deck too hard to sit on. I have no choice but to imagine his legs as they once may have shifted on the back of his donkey on the way to the village, or stamped a shovel into the wet earth. They must have been muscular and deep brown, to match his arms. In the same way, I have no choice but to see my father as a young man jogging after work down Hull Prairie Road. My father and Carlos: two men brought to the ground.

Julia hands me the damp towel and asks me to clean Carlos's wound. I take it cautiously. *He is numb*, she says.

I start to rub vigorously, as if I might be able to scour away poverty, to make a knee appear from the dead end of a stick. I become an archetype of the women who tend men's legs: the nurse who wheels soldiers outside for a smoke; the wife who rubs ointment into the stapled folds of her husband's skin; the little girl who plays with her dolls in the shadow of her father's stump. As I rub, Carlos's raw, tender skin etches his story in every shade of pink and red into the palms of my hands. It's a story of someone branded by diabetes caused by a diet of sugar, because protein is too expensive.

One day, Carlos will crawl on his forearms toward the door like a plant in search of light; one day, my father will drop his beat-up old "sticks" and crumple to the floor. When that moment comes I, too, will lose my legs, to grief.

And so it happens. I wake from a dream that an owl is calling deep in the woods. I know by the way my forearms shake on the blanket that my father is finally dying. He can no longer throw his grandchildren off the dock into the cold Canadian water. He has no leg to stand on. I rush to buy an airline ticket and pack a black dress and heels, just in case. At last, my mother is able to say *Please come*. It is December 30th, 2007. I want to see my father alive.

From the airplane window, I look down at the crosshatched, dried fields of Nebraska. My forehead sweats on the plastic and it is impossible not to be touched by the shape of the creek as it snakes through the field; the solitude of an old barn as we skim over its half-blown-off red roof; or the thoughts of how my father's fourteen grandchildren, my four brothers, his sister, and his wife will all converge on this day. My aunt Emilie in Cambridge folds the laundry and thinks of her brother finally being released from a tortured body. My two brothers together on the golf course in the Dominican Republic tell their favorite story about how Dad hit a hole in one. Grandchildren are still on vacation, throwing snowballs in Vermont. Together, our hearts aim toward a hospital bed in a beautiful glass home in Perrysburg, Ohio, where my father lies covered by a thin white cotton blanket, his mouth open wide, a few strands of silver hair carefully combed across the top of his forehead. Three white tulips stand in a thin bud vase on the bedside table.

When I arrive, the sun is setting behind the bridge on the Maumee River. My mother's shoulders hunch up toward her ears, her lips dry around the edges, as though she can finally utter, *We're here, we're here*. I float down the hall like a feather falling toward death. I kiss my father's pale, purple cheek. I tuck my long fingers into his own and note how matched our bodies are. *Hi, Dad. It's me, Gin. I'm here.*

I swear I see him trying to open his left eye. Through the thin veil of his eyelid he is trying to find me, wanting me to know that he knows I'm there. His kindness is still hardwired into his body. I give him the smile I know he loves, the one that makes my eyes soften and my pupils widen the length of love. With the absolute certainty of a daughter's instinct, I walk to the end of the bed and hold his feet. I pull back the covers and touch his left leg, the bad one. There are no more taboos. I let myself look at his moles and the way the lower part of the leg pitches slightly to the right. I imagine highways of veins crossing behind his knee, his shin purple and red, and the open, weeping wound. His heel, no longer elevated, is finally able to press into the bed, making a dent on the sheet. His leg has carried him all this way, and it is naked and complete. My mother and I find a way to laugh. *Look at the size of his feet!* we say to each other. *Those crazy long yellow toenails*, my mother adds.

I wake at three a.m. to the neon-green, alien light of the clock in my mother's bedroom. I feel a burning, swirling sensation at the top of my head, as if my father is somehow moving through the wall between us, his essence mixing with mine.

By morning, my father's breathing becomes shallow. He is readying himself, like a bird that sings just before it lifts off the branch. We circle him, watching the airway of his mouth and the slight pulsing on the side of his throat. It is the final look on his face. He is utterly relaxed and entirely open, as if the whole world could pass through him: this body that has absorbed a lifetime of food—duck and roasted chickens, mountains of raspberries and chocolate-covered ice cream bars; this body that has stroked the soft, golden fur of thirteen dogs and heard the shrieks of delight from his children and grandchildren playing with frogs by the river; this body, whose shoes have felt the weight of every step on every dirt road and grass and pavement on every continent.

My mother strokes my father's head. *You can go now, Dave*, she says tenderly. *I will be OK. I'll take care of your dog. It's time. You can go now.*

Tears bloom in our eyes. My father stops breathing three times, and each time we lean closer to his mouth, holding our breath in a silent pact to go as far as we can with him. Then a hiccup of air swishes around his pale gray lips. My brother Peter makes us laugh. *He always takes his time. With everything.* And the breathing starts again, the watermark higher in his throat. We all lean back, releasing our air in a collective sigh: a sound he can no longer make.

I hold his feet and touch his leg as he dies. I want to take his legs and feet down the length of my body into the ground underneath me, as something I can always stand on: a legacy.

He exhales, and this time I count inside, waiting for the inhale: *One . . . two . . . three . . . ten. . . .* I wait for life to come back into his mouth. *Eleven . . . twelve . . . thirteen . . . sixteen*: my mother turns toward me, the question in the strained rise of her forehead. *Seventeen . . . eighteen . . . nineteen . . . twenty . . . twenty-one. . . .*

Our skulls feel strangely empty. The clock hums next to the bed. We can hear the high-pitched whine of the electricity in the walls. We look at each other, our chins quivering, our hands reaching. My mother breaks the moment, lightly and inevitably, like the snap of a twig. *He's gone.*

There isn't a death chill in the air. Instead, the bedroom seems too warm. As we rise from our chairs to hug each other, we say nothing, but hold our grief in the fine, thin space between our bodies. It is three o'clock, and the afternoon light is slanting through the archway of the bridge. I leave my red sweater over the white folding chair and we exit the room, in a gesture of finality that doesn't quite know what to do with itself. It's as if we were getting up from dinner at the end of a meal and knew we would never sit at the table together ever again.

We huddle in the kitchen, our bodies needing each other. We eat my father's favorite desserts, chocolate chip cookies and Heath bars. Then, out of the window, I catch sight of a bald eagle flying low and heading west.

I speak to the sky: *There he goes*.

The funeral directors ask my mother if she wants a few minutes with my father before they put him onto the gurney. We line up in the hall for a last look. They wheel him past, tightly wrapped in blankets. He is no longer uncomfortable. His lips and baby-blue eyes are sealed. His gorgeous long hands and feet are tucked out of sight—the signifiers that made Dad, Dad. I watch the bump of his knees jiggle as they pass over the threshold of the front door. His left leg dips over the edge, as if it wants to break free from his pelvis after years of being hauled around. My mouth begins to twitch with the weight of it all, and my tears swallow every arduous step that leg had to make to keep on, keep up, and belong. I stand at the window with Titan, my father's dog, and watch them load Dad's body, head-first, into the beige van. Then he is gone, the bottom of his feet tucked in a cloud. His toes point toward the first star of the night.

That night I have a dream:

> I am running across the street holding Cameron and Brooke's hands. We weave through semitrucks parked at an intersection. A frantic race against the red light, a fleet of tired men hunched

in their cabs. A ragged brown-and-white terrier enters from the left. He dodges tires like a little acrobat leaping this way and that, somehow managing to fly forward. Miraculously, we make it to the other side.

When I wake I want to cry. Three grown women are full of victory against the chase of death. Our hearts are synchronized in heaving, our hands are stiff from clutching onto so much life. We have run so hard. I have wanted to make it all the way with them, and now we have arrived in gulping breaths. I don't know what happens next. Do we stand by the side of the road and hug and kiss each other? Is this a new intersection: Cameron to the left, Brooke to the right, and me down the middle? How perfect that our witnesses are dozens of bleary-eyed men in faded baseball caps.

I think this is when we would laugh, throw our heads back—our long manes of blond hair like three new moons. *It was worth it*, we would say to each other. Brooke would cry, a transparent sleeve of feeling. Cameron would scan the horizon with a still eye.

I would look first to one, then the other, my bare feet placed firmly on the ground and traveling through the dense crust of the earth toward magma. I would feel a powerful surge back through the soles of my feet, a geologic pressure pushing itself against my bare skin as if to say, *Here is where you live. In your feet, where you begin*. This would be my gradient during my time here on earth. I would join all women who love their daughters, their strong legs running, running.

I would like to believe my father is cheering for the women in his life.

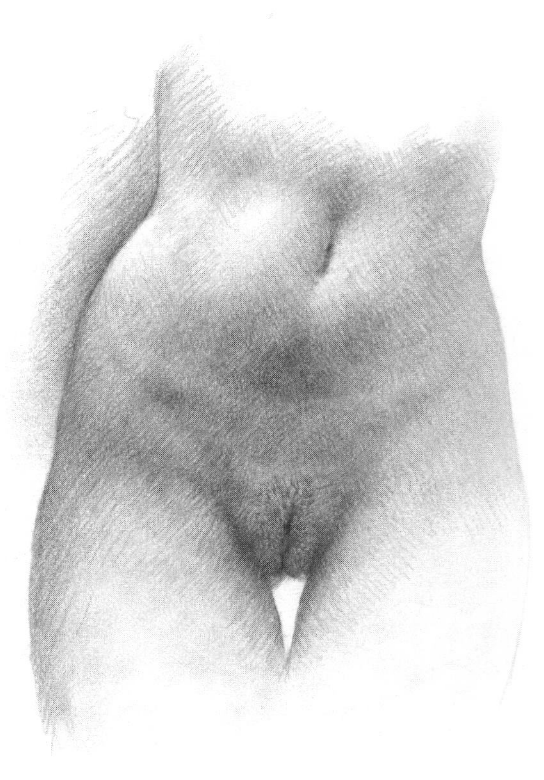

6

VAGINA

VAGINA. I have never liked the sound of the word in my mouth. It rolls around and never seems to come out. It's a word that just lies on the back of the tongue, then swishes around like stale, old beer. It means anatomy, pap smears, plastic scopes, and scraping around. In the American South, it sounds like *vaaaagina*; on the East Coast, it is as punctual and crisp as autumn: *Va-gi-na*. It's an opening that goes nowhere or everywhere, depending upon your emphasis. My high school boyfriend won't use the word. He says *down there*. Great distances are titillating, or so he thinks. I'm not impressed. I tell him *I am right here*. He rolls his eyes in such a way as to say, *I know that*, then he proceeds to paw me to get located. Sometimes my vagina is lonely and vulnerable; sometimes she swims on her own. But she is made to be met: fully and completely.

As a freshman in college I'm excited to go to my first party, especially to meet my friend Chuck's male friends. I cover my right eye with long strips of blond hair, as some kind of primal, sexy defense. I practice smoking cigarettes, using the fumes to flirt, and lowering my hands. But I'm never much good at playing the femme fatale. I grew up with so many brothers and their friends that I don't know how to make the reversal and see a guy as simply material. Girlfriends tell me not to just throw myself on the bed and start chatting. *Don't just squat on the floor and thumb through one of their books*, they say. Apparently, I need to be more mysterious.

One guy, Billy, wants to know what I'm studying. I tell him I love poetry. Silence. He drifts toward the television and I drift toward the door. It's a bitterly cold October night. I walk across campus, along the lit path strewn with soggy leaves, and over Highland Avenue, holding my elbows tightly in my navy pea coat. Suddenly, hands are everywhere. Four guys in military clothes—camouflage pants and black tie-up ankle boots—are grabbing my hair and arms, pushing on my lower back. My sternum heaves. They are throwing me down a ravine. The streetlight tumbles in my vision as I hit the ground and roll backward.

Dark eyes chase me. I hear feet pounding and my clothes ripping. Fingers find my zipper, and my pants are pulled down violently. I feel fingers in my vagina and hear the pant of male fear. Someone screams and screams, and then comes the noise of metal against metal. My throat is stuck open with my own sound. I hear people on the road yelling back. Our voices connect. The four men freak out and scramble up the ravine.

The people on the road are still shouting down into the ravine. I clamp my jaw shut. The tops of the trees seem to freeze. My mind sinks under the weight of so many bodies, and my vagina mutters under her tongue something about closing the door gently when you leave.

Jesus. Are you OK? asks the college couple who were on the road. *Who the hell were those guys? Let me help you get up. Are you sure you are OK?*

They have tender hands and take me back to my room. My roommate is sitting on her bed huddled inside the cocoon of her pink down comforter.

I flush.

She had a close call, the couple tells my roommate. *You might want to report this to the campus police*, they say to me. My roommate sits mute and strangely disbelieving: an innocent horror. I shake myself to sleep and leave the light on.

The police station is painted a drab green, the color of garbage bags. The taxicab driver tells me he is Lebanese, with three children and a wife back home. I start to multiply his story. How many degrees of separation? How many families wrenched apart to make a better life? I duck under the door to his cab and hand him a twenty-dollar bill. *Keep the change for the kids*, I tell him. I stand on the sidewalk, homeless, clutching a black leather purse with a shiny gold catch in the shape of a W. I tell myself, *You'll make a better impression than having a backpack bulging with books*.

I don't know what I'm doing here, but Megan, the dorm resident head, insists. She feels it is important for the sake of all campus women, *for the sake of the female body*.

Our architecture, she exclaims, *is sacred. No one has the right to knock it down, especially down a ravine the first month of college.* Megan's chin quivers and then her eyes go wild. Her hands flail and chop the air, then crush themselves together: lines and then balls of righteous power. My roommate tells me that Megan wants to be an artist.

No one seems to be at the front desk. I slap the metal bell, nipple-shaped and humiliating. A heavyset man introduces himself as Sergeant Moore. When he speaks, his thick black mustache hovers over the edge of his lips like an umbrella. He tells me that the campus police have alerted him as to the nature of my report. He has just a few questions. I sit behind a large, empty metal table and cross my legs. He closes the door. His questions are predictable.

What time was it? Were you drinking? What were you wearing? How many were there? How do you know they were from the military base? Are you sure?

My ankles wrap themselves around each other and I press my heels together.

Now he gets down to details: *Where exactly were they grabbing you? How did they get your pants down? Did they pull off your panties? How many were there again? How many put their fingers in your vagina? Did they have their pants off? When did you start screaming? Who was walking on the road that time of night? Why did they scream back? When did the guys run? Can you identify them?*

I tell Sergeant Moore that I was thrown over backward, that it was after midnight, no moon and the treetops thick. He insists that I come back tomorrow for the lineup.

This time my cab driver is American. He informs me that the Chicago Cubs are having the best year yet. Rain slides down the window. I can't bear to do this—to look at men staring straight at a blank screen, with no blinking allowed. Do they tell these guys who is looking at them through the one-way mirror, that she is shaking so hard she can't keep her legs together? Do they explain to them that she just started college, and that she was so excited to go to a school where no one knew her and she could be anonymous? That this woman is behind a window with a silver glint, studying the enemy, and that I don't know what I'm looking for: the shape of a finger rammed up my vagina. Nonetheless, I attend the lineup and shake my head. *No. Not him. No. Not him. No. Not him.* I don't know what I am doing. The female cop shoves a chair toward me and shuts the door.

On my second journey to Uganda, five women sit on the ground in a circle. They giggle with their hands over their mouths; they can't contain their shyness. I know that, underneath their skirts, some have been circumcised: the adhesions of pain. Suzanna dares to ask: *Do men in America please their wives?* She means: *Do they kiss you, chest to chest—not raped night after night, taken when you lean over to wash off the baby's feet?* She means: *Do your men open you like flowers or like rain falling on the earth?* I don't know how to navigate the gap between truth and brutality. *Some take what they want,* I explain, delicately. *Many take the time to unfold every fold. We must own our bodies,* I continue. *Our fruit must land in our own basket.*

Later on, Florence follows me to the matatu—the wildly

stuffed African bus—her bare feet padding behind me. I stop and smile, and there is a moment of female recognition. Her three-month-old baby is slung on her back. She wants my hand in hers. She confides that she once knew real love, a man who lifted his wings over her. She says he was hacked to death by a machete. His brother escaped. He brought home her man's bloodied hand wrapped in a sandwich bag. I kiss her own hand, as if my love could be enough.

Where is the honoring of women? Inside a torrential thunderstorm on the island of Gozo in the Mediterranean, I dream:

> I am pushing a small brown leather journal, with blank pages the color of onionskin, up my vagina. Blood drips on my finger.

What am I hiding? I can't tell if this is my great secret or a matter of convenience. I think other women at this moment are doing the same thing. We are in on a conspiracy: hidden in caves, water heaving, and blood leaking on the pages. I have everything to say as I walk through the Neolithic temple of Mnajdra on the Island of Malta. The female pubic stone faces the male phallus in the apse of the place of worship built over six thousand years ago. Women know what we now hide.

I travel into the caves under the sanctuary in a blue-and-parrot-green-striped boat painted with the watchful, protective eyes of Osiris. We slowly motor out of the inland sea through the honey-colored limestone caves on the coast. I look up at the ceilings of these great caverns and wonder if a woman's language is hidden here in the spiral scrolls of limestone. I imagine mermaids plunging into the cobalt waters, swimming and sunning themselves, conversing in a forgotten language. I pull my diary from its secret place. I write on the first page: *These mermaids playing. This sea clapping.*

Everything now depends on my vagina. It has to take over the job for my two breasts—to lubricate, get turned on, have an orgasm, and then another. I don't know how to place my body. What position helps me forget they're missing? Does an amputee cover his missing leg with the sheet? Does he prefer to be on top or underneath? Sometimes I keep my t-shirt on or wrap a sarong across my chest. I try to feel sexy, like an exotic dancer. How exactly do you dance into the erogenous when you have no nipples? I discover that you do it by dancing anyway. Your toes and fingertips survive. The body has brushstrokes everywhere.

A friend tells me to celebrate my new body. She says I look like a gorgeous Swedish model, lean and straight. *Like a boy,* I think, *which is what I am not.*

Just get into it, she says, *let your pelvis make up the difference.*

I want to write a book. It would begin with ten basic instructions:

1. Touch her scars. Kiss her as though she has breasts.
2. If she cries, hold her for a very long time.
3. Follow her breath.
4. Begin again.
5. For the first time.

6. Enter her as you would enter a warm lake.
7. If she gets cold, cover her with soft blankets.
8. Keep your eyes open. Take in her whole body.
9. Feed her fire. Deliberately. Specifically.
10. Languish.

I travel once again to Italy, wanting to know how my feet land now in the piazza where the bell tower rings three times. An old Italian man, wearing a navy beret, kisses his fingers and blows them toward the young shopkeeper. I ask myself, *What is the Renaissance in a life? How do I recognize my own harvest?* At dinner, the bottom of the menu at Cibrèo's restaurant reads: *Happiness is an obligation*.

My friend Leslie writes me an e-mail while I'm in Florence. She says the doctor has convinced her that it is time to have her uterus removed. He wants to take her ovaries and cervix while he's at it. She can keep her vagina. I'm the friend who knows about losing body parts. But what language do I speak thousands of miles away in the Internet café next to Giambologna's famous statue *The Rape of the Sabine Women*? Do I resort to syllables of outrage or a gracious *I've been there*? Or do I gesticulate like the Italians, faster than any lips can separate to make a word?

I watch a teenage girl next to me dressed entirely in denim, including a blue-jean-studded beret, rap the computer keys while gabbing to her friend in the next stall. I wonder if she's ever thought about stolen body parts or that it just might be a miracle to reach seventy years old with every part intact. Her universe satellites around any conversation that skips over the fact of loss.

Outside, above her head, the Sabine women are screaming. I've never been able to tell if the look on their faces is terror or ecstasy; the distance between fear and bliss seems only to be a tilt of the head. Today, I decide from the way the afternoon October rain runs down the corridor of the gleaming white Carrara marble that it is rape, unadulterated rape. The men are taking what they want; the women are losing what they will never get back.

The gargantuan statue of Neptune next to the Sabine women was put on a higher pedestal to protect it from further vandalism. Its penis was once stolen, returned, hacked off again, and then reattached. I think of the thousands of statues that have lost limbs in wars: forearms blown into a thousand filaments of marble light; feet cracked and broken while being transported to a local church for refuge; fingers chopped off by an irate Italian fascist after the city was taken by the Allies. The *Winged Victory of Samothrace*—the gorgeous Greek goddess Nike—stands proud without her head and arms. Her hands are encased in glass at the Louvre, her arms and head have never been found. Where are the graveyards for heads, arms, and legs? Surely, Michelangelo's sculptured parts had proper burials. Surely, thousands with immeasurable grief came to the funeral. Surely, they balanced red roses on the marble toes.

I write Leslie: *The loss of your body parts is a big deal.* I tell her that some people's parts get taken, dumped in some surgical trash can on top of the blue paper drapes and latex gloves. Or some are sent to the lab for further inspection, and a lab technician numbers the parts for identification. Then they are chopped and sliced, and the blood is wiped up until all that is left is filleted tissue. There is no mention of a woman named Leslie, or that she has loved dozens of young children into adulthood.

I advise her to start talking, if only to the pitcher on the table that reminds her of her grandmother's hands. *Stay up late*, I write, *for as long as it takes to say everything.* I tell her that the night before I lost my first breast I got on my knees and held on to the metal frame of my bed for dear life. Terror latched on to me and I felt my naked breasts falling onto the floor. I told her I wailed into the wool carpet, with my mouth frozen open, until my face was soaked. I stayed up late and said everything to Roger, until the horror finally slid off my face.

Leslie, I can say, *the body knows wholeness as the last thing it puts to bed at night. A body can't separate from itself. When your uterus is gone it will rise and fall. It will make sleep sounds. It will turn over with the rest of you.*

The signs are suspicious. The cells in my mother's uterine lining are changing. As if they'd altered their personality after all these years, they have become aggressive. My mother has a hysterectomy. They drag her womb out through her vagina like pulling a balloon through its own neck. The womb that bore me, the first lake in which I swam, lies in the doctor's hands. I speak to my mother on the phone, as she puts words together through a tube of after-drugs. She says she's angry: *They couldn't get my ovaries*. She wants them out, just in case. *I've had it with cancer in this family*.

Ten years after my mother has a hysterectomy, the physicians tell me I, too, should have my uterus removed along with my ovaries, *just in case*. Like my mother, I am furious. It feels they are taking the kitchen sink, as well as all the plumbing.

I write my uterus a letter:

I have been meaning to write you this thank-you note. Our relationship ended a long time ago. After Brooke was born, the winter of '87. The ice on Left Hand Creek was so thick I walked over to the Woods' house to borrow an extension cord for the electric heater in the back bedroom. It was so cold that day I wore two Irish fisherman sweaters the way my grandmother used to, one hem rolled over the other.

Thank you for making room for three extraordinary children. A room for each, spacious enough to allow them to bounce around, kick the walls. You never complained. You got bigger than any situation. You housed the great gifts of my life and never asked for anything in return. Then opened the strings of your silk purse and spilled at the perfect moment. Not too soon.

Not too late.

I knew it was over when Brooke took her place. I used to think of you as a burlap bag, relatively useless. Your job done. Blood collecting in you and spewing out. For months I forgot about you.

You slid back into place. Hidden in the cave behind my pubic bone. No one else took up residence when you became melancholic.

What creative use will we have for each other now?

I hope the rest of my life will be the answer.

7

EAR

FRIENDS GIVE ME pairs of huge dangling earrings. They tell me my ears are one of my best features, that I have earlobes shaped like opals. I am being told my ears will make up for my breasts. I am determined to make myself beautiful, anyway.

In first grade, sitting in our new breakfast nook, on an orange, half-moon-shaped bench, I wait for my toast. My saddle shoes swing above the floor. Instead of toast, however, my mother, cocooned in her plaid flannel nightgown, makes me eat canned pears soaked in heavy syrup. She says that pears help with constipation. I don't even know what constipation means. She seems focused on my body parts: how long my legs are growing, if my fingernails are turning yellow.

What's that red spot behind your knee? she asks. When it comes to ears, all my mother can say is they are things to clean out like the drain in the kitchen sink. She tells me that all day we collect debris. On the playground that afternoon, I hear a smack against my ear and then the singing of wings. Something is crawling in my ear. I get my friend Cynny to look inside, and she screams, *There's a beetle in there!* My teacher takes me to the infirmary and the nurse tells me to stop crying.

My bedroom is the farthest away from my parents'. I think they want me to feel special, as if I have my own girl-place. My mother redecorates it for me. *More up-to-date*, she says. I'm seven years old and I don't have a clue about the color wheel. It's late at night and I'm running down the long hall cupping my ear in the palm of my sweating hand. I'm in pain and I need my mother. *Mom*, I whisper. I don't dare touch her. Somehow I know it's the golden rule never to wake my parents unless it is an absolute emergency. I scan the mental list: bleeding, throwing up, broken bones. These are serious enough for my mother's sleep to be interrupted. But what about pain deep inside the tunnel of your ear—an on-fire pain, a pressure-dive pain?

My mother wakes. Her hands rush to the lights; covers are thrown off; her beige silk nightgown sweeps the floor. Tears slice my cheeks as the visible sign of the hot, searing knife that is cutting my ear. I can't stop. Dad calls Dr. Frasier. Mom gets the hot compress, the Children's Tylenol. When the doctor arrives I am a fetus, curled against my pillow. *A punctured eardrum*, he announces. *She's too young for this. Something is wrong with her ears.*

Later, I discover my ears can be tunnels of sexual bliss. I'm thirteen and Roland has been my knight since first grade. He loves to hold my hand and read Thoreau out loud. He meets me in the alley and we play four-square, the yellow chalk lines faded from the snow. He plays dare with the ball, faking throw after throw until he hits me in the shins. I fall to the ground pretending to be devastated, and he scoops me up. He kisses my entire face—my cheeks, forehead, eyelids, eyebrows, the little point of my chin, my jaw, the corner of my lips, and then finally my ears. I discover what it means to stop breathing.

My roommates in boarding school—Tanya, Sheila, and Leila—talk me through the piercing. First, they numb one ear at a time with ice, then they sterilize the needle by burning it with a match. I squeeze Tanya's hand while Sheila stabs my ear. This is my first real act of rebellion. My mother had always told me to wait until I got older, *just to be sure*, and that I should, *for God's sake, do it professionally*. But I want to join the ranks of exotic women. Sheila tells me to start buying earrings. *Some crazy American woman from Pennsylvania won the Guinness Book of Records for owning the most pairs of earrings*, she announces in awe: *17,122*. We calculate: according to these numbers it would take fifty years to wear a new pair every day.

Teaching childbirth classes is my way of having fifty babies. I'm twenty-four, newly married, and trying to have one of my own.

The mothers, followed by dutiful husbands, waddle across my redwood deck in their voluminous corduroy jumpers for evening class. Their weight makes the kitchen shimmy. The truth is I love each and every one of them.

I demonstrate with my ear. I place it on a volunteer's belly and pause for a long time. *This is how the midwives used to listen*, I say. We try to guess the difference between a boy- and a girl-wave: the movement of tides. I explain that the next development in listening to a fetus was the horn device, whereby you placed your ear on one end and cupped the other end on the belly. From there, medicine progressed to the stethoscope, where you put the plastic ends in your ears and the cold metal disc on the stomach. From the stethoscope, medicine moved to the fetal heart monitor, where you were wheeled into a room, sticky goo was rubbed on your abdomen, and electrodes were stuck to your body above the pubic line.

I tell the husbands to kneel at their wives' sides, pull up their dresses, and place their ears on their wives' bellies. *Do you hear your seed?* I ask.

I want to run around and put my ear to everything, to experience the unborn falling out of my ear.

I write to the children in my journal:

Taylor,

When you are born you are all ears. Wildly shaped spinnakers. We tease you, wonder what planet you come from. My guess Pluto, the far-reaching orb whose citizens have to lean all the way over to hear the muttering of planet Earth. Long, beautifully open ears stretching all the way to the ground. You cry a lot. More than you sleep or daydream. You cry at every noisy intrusion. The telephone, the dropped saucepan. Your ears are on fire.

It is silence you love. Perfect planetary space. Like the dust balls floating over your crib, you want to watch and listen. Instructions from above on how to be in a body. Your birth isn't exceptional. No violence, just the long hours looping over themselves with exhaustion and bewilderment. I cry for perfection. I cry for your face. I cry and cry. You spill out in water and blood and are perfect. Even those gorgeous giant ears have their place. I whisper into them every language of welcome I know. Little Taylor, you will grow into those ears of yours. Soon enough you will be a man who can take it all, the engine roar, the noisy party, the rough speech of this world. But for now let those translucent ears with their tiny red veins be the antennae to whatever star you fell from.

Cameron,

At three years old, you slosh your words and we can't understand you. The doctor says you need tubes in your ears. When the surgeon takes you in his arms you scream and grab on to my neck. Terror latches on. And I hold you for a moment as tight as I can.

Brooke,

Your ears are round, a spiral flower. Utterly perfect.

. . .

I am sitting in a café as busloads of tourists, like ants in t-shirts, climb the fountain in the piazza in Assisi, Italy. The fountain's large rectangular stone inlay is in proportion to its saint. For the next ten days, I will walk in the footsteps of St. Francis, from Assisi to the meditation caves on Monte Subasio, to Perugia, Gubbio, and finally, Mount Vernon. I want to lay my heel inside of the saint's.

On the train from Assisi back to Florence I fall to the floor. The backs of the train seats pick themselves up and throw themselves sideways. The brown plastic light fixture whirls and I grab my suitcase on the way down. A ringing sound gouges my ear. I cry out to anyone and close my eyes to get it to stop. The red violence grabs my eyelids and shakes them. I claw the floor, my hands trying to get the world to hold still. I make out the bloated face of a woman looking down at me. Her head is spinning. She is mouthing something about being drunk. She leans over and I grab her neck. Terror latches on, like Cameron as a child. I crawl off the train, the woman carrying my suitcase. I try to stand by holding the stone wall, coaching myself just to make it to the taxi. I ask the cab driver to take out my wallet and look for the folded piece of paper that has my friend's address on it. *Please take me there* I say. *I don't know what's happening to me.*

I have an electronystagmography (ENG) test. I am placed in a dark room with electrodes near my eyes. I feel warm and then cold water circulating in my ears. The technician reassures me that the vertigo will last only twenty seconds. I scream, flailing for her hand. My eyes bulge and my eyelids flick.

You are going deaf, the doctor says, *and have very poor balance function on the right side*. It's confirmed: I have Ménière's disease, named after Prosper Ménière, a French physician. He observed deaf-mute patients in Paris in 1861 and noticed other patients suffering symptoms of hearing loss and vertigo, and the medical world listened to him. He had already won the Knight of Legions Award for his leadership against the cholera epidemic in southern France. I try to link the history of my ear with Ménière's biography. I discover that he was a prolific writer on subjects as diverse as medicine, botany, the Roman poets, and Cicero. There it is, I realize. He and I share a poetic ear.

That's not the only thing I share. My mother and my grandmother also have Ménière's disease. My mother can hear a silent dog whistle—one of the strange capacities of losing the lower octaves of hearing. She tells me that her last bad attack was when she was pregnant with me. I wonder what this means. Did I spin around in my amniotic home, grabbing onto my umbilical cord for dear life? A friend suggests that it's karma. She says I have the power to end this female inheritance and save my daughters. Another friend tells me that her uncle suffered from it so badly that he spent years in bed. She thinks this was his way of avoiding his overbearing wife. The Chinese acupuncturist says the ear is connected to the intestines. The ear, nose, and throat doctor assures me that I am experiencing an autoimmune disease. The endocrinologist believes that I have a hormone problem related to fluid retention. A spiritual teacher says it is the ultimate lesson: that we never had control over our lives to begin with. I tell myself that if I can just find the right switch to pull, I can stop it.

Dr. Thompson asks me if I know I share the disease with Vincent Van Gogh. He points to the print of *Starry Night* on his office wall and tells me he spent two years reading all of Vincent's letters to his brother Theo. They describe the exact symptoms of Ménière's disease: violent vertigo; a loud, chronic ringing in the ear; deafness; uncontrollable vomiting; despair.

I write Vincent a letter.

Dear Vincent,

I have always wondered about your ears pinned under that straw hat. What colors they must have heard. Running like rivers through nautilus apertures into the haunt of your eyes. Cadmium yellow. Vermilion. Your fields sing of it. But what was mixing itself in the alchemy at night, while vertigo hung your sanity like a bat for days? People say you were crazy, cutting off your ear. Raving for saints and full of black passions.

Please just keep painting. For both of us.

I drive Taylor to the airport in Denver. It is his first trip to Europe and we are both excited. Less than halfway down Highway 36 the familiar sensation starts in the middle of my brain. The road starts to tip up and then to the right. The car in front of me turns sideways and the white cumulus clouds devour the sky. *Taylor,* I say, *I've got to pull over.* I am folding into myself, trying to come up with a strategy. I feel the panic, the sense that there is no exit from this experience. I hold my head in my hands and push back into the leather seat. Taylor takes the wheel and doesn't say a word. He is devotion itself. I tell him to pull up to the curb at Departures, get a policeman, and then run to the gate. *Tay, don't worry about me,* I add. *I'll be fine. Taylor, you really need to go.*

He gently kisses me goodbye on the forehead. This is supposed to be his moment, not mine. I can't even open my eyes to get a last look at him. I explain to the cop that I have a disease called Ménière's and soon I won't be able to move or see or hear. I refuse the tears that are beginning to pressure the inside corners of my eyes. The cop leaves to get the nurse from the airport hospital. *Please, don't leave me here*, I plead to the steering wheel.

The medics pull a wheelchair to the car door and slide me into it as carefully as they would a box full of breakables and wheel me into the bowels of the airport. I hear the ding of the elevator and feel myself turning right and left. With my eyes closed, I could be anywhere. We arrive at the airport hospital, a place I never knew existed. I hear two men discussing Flight 307 rerouting to Denver because a woman on board has had a heart attack. I grab on to the chance to get outside of myself and become fascinated. I join the family of crisis: a woman rerouted so we can meet.

I coach the nurse to get the shot of zincum valerian out of my purse. She tells me that she can't give it to me, that it would be medical malpractice. *OK, then you will have to fill the shot and hand it to me*, I say. *Help me aim it just above the tattoo on my right butt cheek.* I can't open my eyes. *I need to get it in quick before I start vomiting*. Finally, the needle is inserted and the fix begins to work. The world starts to slow down, as if every object is going home. I decide that this is what a heroin addict must feel like. My body rejoins itself and the metal chair next to the bed tips back upright. I hear a tall male nurse say: *Let's get the gurney ready for the heart attack victim*.

My life is pitched toward exits. If I have an attack, how will I make it to the bed? How will I get out of the movie theater and into the car? Driving becomes strategies of U-turns and one-ways. Finally, I have to stop. The anxiety of being alone or with my three children in a 3,400-pound machine, with the possibility of the road picking itself up, does me in. Taylor wants to know when this is going to end. When will I be able to scramble the eggs without holding on to the side of the counter? Roger doesn't know what to do. He starts to spend more time in his studio.

The dictionary says that gravity is the natural force of attraction exerted by a celestial body, such as earth, upon objects at or near its surface, tending to draw them toward the center of the body. Actually, losing gravity is like being thrown to the center of the planet, thrashing and grabbing on to anything solid on the way down: the bedpost, the stainless-steel throw-up bowl, my own hand. Where is the center in a room that is whirling at twenty miles per hour? Having no gravity in outer space is called *dance*. Having no gravity on earth is called *violence*.

I've lost count of the days passed in that lower atmosphere where illness collides with my body. Nothing can be done; I seem to be floating . . . somewhere. If I could walk I would stretch out my hands, like a blind woman listening for light. Pitched toward suffering, toward the old and paralyzed, I want to ask what these people know of darkness and if it lasts forever.

At the end of every bad attack, when the drugs finally kick in, I feel buoyant and unexpectedly peaceful. I fall into the eye of the storm, where I am suspended in a luminous sky; my lips feel far below me. This is when I have conversations with the dead. Cathy and Justin are here, Amethyst, too. We are exchanging air; their last breaths are inside me. They say that being dead is like floating on a pond, looking up at the clouds traveling to their places.

Cathy tells me that there is no such thing as *taking a life*. She explains that the cancer in her lungs had already stolen the faces of her unborn grandchildren. She wants me to know that she had to take the pills alone, that this was her choice. She knew I was sitting on the bed in my red kimono.

Amethyst says that she never believed that leukemia was a killer who would sneak in her bedroom in the middle of the night and draw chalk around her body. Instead, she thought it was an ally who sat by her bed trying to make her live her life more fully. She asks me to be a good mother to her children. She thanks me for sharing my dream with her kids of her sailing away on a huge white swan.

Justin always shows me the same thing: how he wasn't alone when he died, and how a beautiful angel reached under the car and pulled him out and laid him down by a tree; how the angel stepped behind him and reached under his armpits and pulled him out of his body; how he kept holding on to him when the ambulance came.

I want to tell Cathy, Amethyst, and Justin that I am barely making it, that I am stuck between worlds that have no horizons, with no sunrise or sunset, that I am in what Dante means by purgatory. I want to tell all of them that I remember the light, but I don't know how to reach it.

. . .

On an overcast winter morning Roger drives me to a new ear, nose, and throat doctor. A friend of a friend says that Dr. Stanley is great. She says he has a soul that *shines like a new penny*. This time Roger stays in the car and reads a Buddhist text. I always hate the period when I meet a new physician where I have to relate my history. I try to run through the onset of the disease and each occurrence of it as quickly as I can. My shield is to tell the facts without feeling. Meanwhile, the Doc sits on a rolling stool, scuttles across the room like a crab, and shows me plastic models of the inside of the inner ear. Then he scurries back to his desk and scribbles pages of notes on white lined paper. Meanwhile, I am looking for his soul. *Complicated,* he mutters. *We don't really know what causes Ménière's disease.*

The human ear is full of tools—anvils, hammers, and stirrups—but apparently I have no idea how to use them. The inner ear—the portion that is located within the temporal bone and is involved in both hearing and balance and includes the semicircular canals, vestibule, and cochlea—is also called *the labyrinth.* It's a perfect name for the inner pathways and tunnels that determine whether I can get out of bed, lean over to put on my jeans, or pour Brooke's cereal. These beautiful delicate ears can't seem to find the single path leading to the center. I receive partial answers and leave the doctor's clutching a white prescription sheet for Ativan, *to help with the anxiety.* Snow falls on the windshield. Roger, head bent, looks like he is praying.

The middle ear is the space between the eardrum and the inner ear that contains the three auditory ossicles, which convey vibrations through the oval window to the cochlea. I consider the space between my bed and the bathroom; between a dream about a flying lynx and a nightmare that I am being chased by a rabid dog; between four a.m. and six a.m. when I can't sleep; between morning and noon vitamins; between phone calls to and from the doctor and the kingfisher landing on the bird feeder. My love for these spaces is growing. They feel to me like resting grounds, knolls I can sit on and steady myself before the grass tips over.

The outer ear is that portion that includes the auricle and the passage to the eardrum. I imagine the passage is like the Grand Canyon and my outer ear is the collar of stone that calls me all the way down. I want to believe that first light slides down their slick faces, over the rim and down the shadowy hole. I want to believe there will always be chamber music.

The one compensation is that my earlobes are long, like those of the women in the ancient myths of China and India whose lobes were revered as a sign of wisdom. All ears are unique and rival fingerprinting as a form of identification. I want to make a map of my ear on parchment paper, with chambers drawn like vases and with gardens of fine hair and circular canals with azure-blue water. I want to roll the parchment up and seal it with earwax and place it under my pillow. Perhaps I will dream that my ear sleeps free of this earth and that it will have an afterlife.

. . .

I opt for the endolymphatic shunt. Dr. Thompson hands me a printout:

> The operation consists of opening the mastoid bone of the skull and identifying the endolymphatic sac, which is located in the posterior fossa dura. To find the sac, the sigmoid sinus is denuded of its bony cover except for a small rectangle of thin bone. The sigmoid sinus is then collapsed with gentle pressure and the sac exposed behind the posterior semi-circular canal. The sac is then incised and the shunt tube is inserted. It is a one-way valve that allows fluid to flow out.

I underline, *identifying, denuded, collapsed.* I picture an old tenement building. My ear was identified as failing and denuded and then collapsed. Dr. Thompson tells me that he wants to check the pressure against my eardrum. He is going to place a tiny valve into the inner ear chamber to regulate the fluid. *The amount of fluid is so minuscule you barely see it with the naked eye*, he says. *All this havoc from a drop of water.*

While the nurse is prepping me for ear surgery, I ask her to tell me exactly what I just signed. She tells me that there is a possibility that the surgeon could nick a nerve that controls the facial muscles. *If for any reason he does*, she says, *your face will fall several inches on your right side.* It's a risky business, to look like I've had a stroke at the age of forty-five. The nurse shows me the spot behind my ear where the surgeons will drill a quarter-sized hole to reach the inner ear. *He can't go through the eardrum, darling*, she continues, *or you'd go deaf. You'll be under about five hours. You can expect the worst of the vertigo to last three or four days.* The nurse puts her hand behind her own ear and tells me the hole will make it hard to adjust my sunglasses.

Proudly, the doctor tells me the device they will use is his own invention. I resent the fact that all these doctors who have diseases, tools, and procedures named after them are male: Dr. William House, Dr. Ménière. These are their progeny, which will outlive them for centuries. *Where are the women?*

I dream:

> An ancient old man wrapped in a dark cloak takes me down into a stone chamber. There are ceiling-high bookshelves, dusted with a fine white powder. I sit at a large oak desk while the old man reaches for a leather-bound volume as wide as the palm of his hand. He reads, *Ménière's is on the Most Dreaded Disease List. In the top five.* He turns the page, blowing powder into the air. He reads, *Ménière's is on the Most Sacred Disease List. In the top five.*

I try to connect *sacred* with *dread*. It's like connecting heaven with hell. I am aware that something does happen in the long hours of an actual attack. A veil parts above my face as if to help the sun reach my forehead and keep me in this world. Strangely, there is something sacred about knowing that we never really have total control. Over anything.

I volunteer at the hospital, sitting on the bed with Helen, an elderly woman whose skin is like an onion peel. She is dying of a rare blood disease. I check the tiny corners of her eyes, now the color of translucent milk. A pool begins to spill over the crest of her nose. The leaflet on my lap reads, *In the final hours the eyes can tear,* and I wonder what other valleys live in her body—the triangle of her armpit, her thinly scooped elbows—and if these, too, fill with water salted from life. And is water the last sorrow, or just the way the body remembers the ocean? Helen once told me her illness was the great gift of her life. But I want to know about salvation.

My friend Max tells me about trepanation or trepanning. It is the oldest surgery known to man; indeed, archeologists have found 120 prehistoric skulls in southern France with holes drilled into them. The idea was that a door for the Spirits was made where they could enter and speak to you. It was where you seeped out when you died. The thought gives me comfort: that the hole in my skull is for the messages from Spirits.

With the surgery over, I look like a war casualty. Thick, flesh-colored bandages are wrapped under my chin and over my right ear. I can't move my head, not even an inch. The vertigo, the promised burning, is putting out the lights. *Kids, don't move near me,* I beg. *Don't sit on the bed.* In the Navaho myth of the Ear-Sleeper, the large-eared dwarfs use their ears as bedding: one ear as a mattress, the other as a coverlet. I have to sleep sitting up for six weeks, the pillows arranged in a throne behind, to the side, and under me. I feel slightly important. Friends bring me chocolate cake. Lying down has never been sweeter. In my sleep, I manage to slide down my feathered chair of pillows until I am almost flat. My body is faithfully in love with gravity.

The return to life is slow: I don't want to move fast anywhere. Feeding the dog is enough; so is pouring water on the ficus tree.

I begin to trust my ear, just as I trust the car radio to keep on playing. I am desperate to get outside of myself, to feel the simple pleasure of driving to the post office to get stamps. Cameron tells me she dreamed that she had her ears pierced with blue rhinestone studs. I move past archaic ideas that my daughter should wait until she is old enough. Ears are becoming sacred. Besides, I believe in dreams. I drive that very afternoon for the first time in six months to the little booth at the mall. In her red cotton miniskirt, Cameron sits on the tall stool and holds my hand while a gun punches a hole in her ear.

Five years later, in the late fall, when the leaves on the cottonwoods are dancing their brightest yellow, I take a hot tub down by the creek. My friend David and I talk about the future, how we want to spend more time in the sea. When I lean over to pull myself out, I crash to the ground. I hear the scream from both of us as I cling to the earth. A white terror fills my head. Leaves streak out of control against the sky. The doctor says it is called a *drop attack*, technically an *otolithic crisis of Tumarkin*. The valve is no longer working; it is clogged like leaves in a gutter. In effect, my ear is dying.

I choose the gentamicin drip. I will receive another hole, a tiny one whose width is a little hope. My eardrum will be punctured to inject a toxic drug into my inner ear in order to destroy the nerve. It will be another death by poison. The hole will close up after a few days, but, Dr. Smith tells me, it may take three or four treatments to do the job. He tells me I have a good chance of going deaf in my right ear.

The morning before the procedure I write a poem.

Deaf

The shadows of love slip
through the walls
I cannot sleep.
God says, *Give me your ear*
I cry, *What kind of love is this?*
Meanwhile the waves reach higher,
the moon skates out of sight.

All night I burn, refuse the price,
loss of bell ringing, creek singing, wind tossing
for an astonished silence
taken not given.
I cling to the other ear
like a child to a blanket
praise the perfection of pairs,
eyes and hands and ears
while the night sounds muffle
then go dead.

And in my final surrender
the soft waves of sleep
rinse my ear
as deaf as a white stone
washed up on the beach.

The day after the doctor injects my inner ear, my heart pounds in its cave. The vase of pink roses drifts sideways and the cottonwood outside the bedroom splits in two, then four, then eight, and then rotates. Dr. Smith tells me this is normal when one loses one's balance function. The word he uses, *function*, feels utterly wrong for this loss. It seems to me more like *certainty*, *poise*, *backbone*. As for the double vision, Dr. Smith tells me it lasts only six months. I splay my hands open and count the number of palms. The sole ceiling fan above me moves clockwise, at secondhand speed.

I look up at the top of Huayna Picchu, the mountain towering above Machu Picchu, and see a dozen or so people above me, small dots against an Andean sky. The clouds wrap around the back peak. It is only seven months since my ear was killed, three months since I had to learn to walk all over again. My children watch me crawl from the bedroom to the bathroom, pushing my hand against the wall to turn the corner. I tell them not to laugh, that they looked as funny when they were first learning to scoot. And now here I am, at nine thousand feet. They say that when you look down on the Incan site of Machu Picchu, the place resembles a puma.

You can do this, my friends cheer. I have no idea how. All I have to go on is the doctor's pep talk about how the human brain is a miracle, how it knows how to compensate for the loss of balance on one side. Somehow, I am told, the brain figures things out and tips the world upright. But the doctor didn't say anything about climbing two thousand feet straight up, a StairMaster of stone and sheer cliffs.

Each step is my miracle. Friends take turns leaning me away from the edge. A hundred yards from the top I have to make a choice: do I squeeze through a tight tunnel of jagged rocks or walk the long way around? I opt for my birth. As I emerge through the tunnel, my right calf gets stuck. I pull harder and an intense pain shoots down my leg. The hole is too small. My friends, now my midwives, encourage me to take a rest, breathe deeply, and call on the spirits of the mountains.

I start to cry tears that have been waiting for years to spill, pouring grief all over my dark shirt. I cry for all the hard work of staying upright, for every mealtime with my family when the world was moving and gelatinous and I faked being there. My tears and my friends' soft faces and the thin blue sky are suddenly a wave on this high reef that carries me through. Miraculously, my leg slides and I fall back, exhausted under the powerful sun. My laughter arrives with the breeze on top of Huayna Picchu.

I start climbing new mountains inside me. *What if? What if?* I chant to myself. *What if I help raise funds to build a medical clinic in a remote village in the Andes?* Surely these impoverished voices deserve to be heard. *What if hundreds of Peruvian children are spared the pain of a simple ear infection?* I take the chance and little eight-year-old Pedro receives antibiotics. *What if I take my children to Uganda to work alongside my doctor friend to help women with HIV?* I take the chance. When I pass a boy walking down a fly-infested dirt road in the refugee camp in Uganda, I turn around and look again. Both of his ears have been cut off. He is a victim of the knife of Joseph Kony, the leader of the Lord's Resistance Army. I can't take my eyes off the knobs of flesh hanging like onion bulbs from the sides of his head. I don't know how to go back and hug him. I walk a tightrope between fury and tenderness. I am sick of this sickness.

I become a left-sided person. I remind my friends where to speak. I point to my left ear: *This is my good ear,* I say when we take a walk. It's irritating to keep reminding people. I think to myself, *Will they only remember when I'm eighty?* I start hating loud restaurants; the volume is like a crowd scene in a bad movie. I can't follow the curve of my own voice. On top of it, I'm stuck pitched to the person on my left. So much depends on my left ear.

My ears ring and have done so ever since I can remember. Some days the sound is the language of birdsong or wind among the treetops, the roar of beasts. Some days, I hear the military on the march. When these sounds become unbearable, I bury my ear under a stack of pillows and dream of an underground river. Now I have the greatest excuse for silence in the world: *I'm sorry, I can't hear you.* People sound as though someone stuffed a plastic bag over their mouths: *Let's listen to the creek, instead,* I say. *No, Mom. I didn't say put the clothes in the dryer,* Taylor laughs. *I said the car has a flat tire.*

I volunteer at Boulder Community Hospital to test the hearing of babies. I want to hold on to the promise symbolized by the blue-and-pink blankets. The staff trains me to attach the tiny electrodes to the nape of the infants' necks and temples, to read the data, and to tell the parents the results. In the U.S., approximately one in a thousand newborns, or an average of thirty-three babies every day, are born profoundly deaf. Another two to three of those thousand babies are born with partial hearing loss. Every such child who doesn't receive early intervention will have a lifetime medical cost of one million dollars.

A deaf couple asks that their baby be tested in their room instead of the nursery. They want to receive the news in private. I wheel the machine into the room. The baby is asleep in the bassinet with a pink card. Her name is Angela. I'm not sure how to greet this couple. The husband, dressed impeccably in a yellow cable sweater and ironed blue jeans, sits on the side of the bed. His dark-haired wife's eyelashes are slightly wet. I am awkward with my hands. They twirl and then drop the green sheet of paper that explains the hearing test procedure.

My heart climbs the question of what news would be better for a deaf couple: to have their baby hear or not? I attach the electrodes while looking up and smiling at the mother. I try to tell her with my entire body that it will be fine: *Your baby girl is beautiful. You are so brave.* Angela has ten fingers and toes, a head of black curly hair, and rosebud lips. She squirms as I pull off the tape. I raise my thumb to tell her parents: she has perfect hearing in both ears. They hold on to each other. As I shut the door, I can hear the sound of crying.

In a bat storm, in a cave or at night, a single bat can know its own sound among thousands of its flying neighbors. It can detect its signals even if they are two thousand times fainter than the background noises. A bat's entire auditory system weighs a fraction of a gram. Ounce for ounce, watt for watt, the system is millions of times more efficient and more sensitive than humankind's invention of radars.

As for me, I try different hearing aids. The audiologist explains that since I am virtually deaf on the right side I'm a good candidate for the BAHA, the Bone-Anchored Hearing Aid. *It's the latest*, she tells me. It will require a simple outpatient procedure in which a hole will be drilled into my skull, behind the right ear, and a titanium screw implanted. A hearing device will then be snapped onto the screw and in a split second the sound from my good ear will conduct through the bone. I imagine my skull as a sky becoming full of black holes. I've had enough of drilling. Instead, I choose a new, computer-synched model that rests in the bowl of my ear. *It's discreet*, says the audiologist, *and comes in four shades of gray, two in brown, or a basic black*.

At my next appointment, Dr. Smith tells me that there is a 10 to 40 percent possibility of bilateral Ménière's. *It tends to be higher with women*, he says. I hold my breath. A river of fear passes through me. Dr. Smith's hands look like stalks of wheat blowing over the papers on his desk. His feet rock; the white paper sheet crackles. I reassure myself, *It will not be me*.

A friend tells me that in Egypt, in the middle of the eastern wall that surrounds the great Temple of Amun, is the Chapel of the Hearing Ears. The ancient reliefs are called *ear stelae*, left and right profiles of perfect tiny raised ears. These ears are engraved as a dedication to the Gods for answered prayers. Inspired, I write my own dedication to my left ear:

Thank you for helping me walk in a straight line.
Thank you for helping me reach the apple on my tree.
Thank you for my children's voices.
Thank you for the adventure books. Of falling snow and lightning.

On the way to lunch with my friend Jacob, I run back into the house and take an allergy pill on my bedside table. Halfway down the highway that leads to Boulder, the cars in front of me start dividing into two. I am strangely detached, curious. *How do they do this?* I wonder. I continue to drive, noticing that my fingers seem much larger than I remember. In fact, my thumb is the size of a large carrot. *How bizarre!* I think. I stop at a red light and gently bump into the car's rear end ahead of me. A woman gets out and examines her car. She waves to me that all is OK and climbs back in her vehicle. When I arrive at the restaurant, I accidentally pull up on the sidewalk and hit the parking meter. With heavy legs and in slow motion I go to find Jacob. *Something is wrong,* I tell him. *Take me to the hospital.* As we drive, I tell Jacob that I might be experiencing Ménière's again. How could this be? It doesn't usually happen like this. I always have enough awareness to pull over and make a call on my cell. *It's been years,* I mutter.

The MRI of my brain shows there are a multitude of white spots of demineralization. The neurologist comes into the emergency room and tells me that it is hard to interpret this display of white matter. The MRI film looks like clusters of snow laced over the top of two gray-and-white folded bulges. He goes through the symptom checklist. I don't have the symptoms of multiple sclerosis; I don't have neurological fallout. He signs me out of the hospital and tells me that I might want to see a specialist.

Two days later, I notice the prescription bottle of Ambien on my nightstand next to the allergy bottle. The awareness drops into my head like sunlight striking a crystal ball: *My God, I drove on a sleeping pill. I drove inside of a dream!* Do I howl in laughter or marvel?

After this "dream drive," I begin to think that what is happening with my body is much like clouds passing across the sky. Here one minute, gone the next. A wise friend and I conclude over breakfast together: when you lose precious things, like body parts, don't you unconsciously look for what was lost? And if you search, don't you lose yourself in the searching? And if you lose yourself in the search, don't you feel as though you have no edges? You feel like running water. And eventually you become the thing you were searching for: A wholeness that isn't dependent upon the body.

I think of how many times I told the kids fairy tales about the quest for the Holy Grail and how you have to leave home and go into the woods and face horrible demons, only to come home and find the very thing you are looking for under the bed.

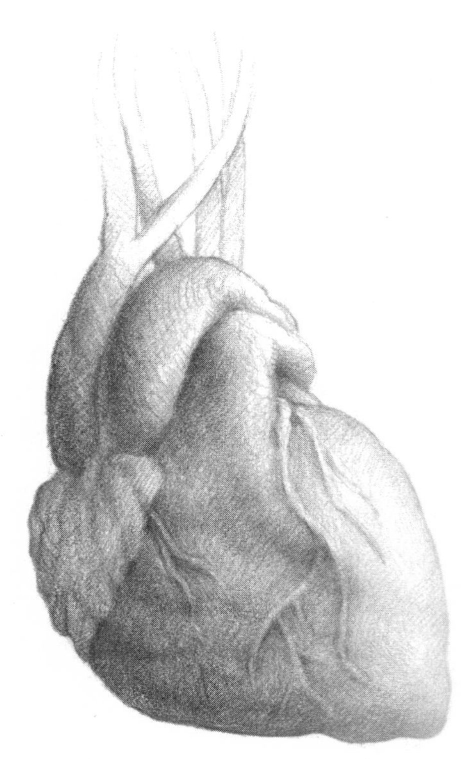

8

HEART

A NURSE, who is originally from Mexico City, tells me that an EKG of the heart on a woman with a mastectomy can be interpreted as a bit irregular. *Don't worry. I see it all the time*, she says as she sticks electrodes on my sternum. I press my right palm just above my heart. I have no breast tissue left to squish, nothing to push through. All that remains is this paper-thin membrane of skin that I can pull away from my chest wall with a slight tug of my thumb and index fingers. I can't decide if it is a gain or loss—to feel my heart just on the other side of my skin, so close that I could reach in and pluck it, like a pear.

I dream:

> People point at me as I walk down the sidewalk. I don't realize I am naked until I enter a teashop. I have no shoes. I have no pants, no sweater, no jacket, or hat. People smile. I try to cover up with napkins. But my heart lights up the paper. My heart is beaming like a lighthouse and pulsing a pink-red light like ET.

I am losing heart, and so is Roger. He stays in his studio, late into the night. The sounds of Paul McCartney sidle out of the window. Above us, the moon turns yellow. I begin to hide my illness under the covers, even under the bed. Illness takes up all three shelves of the medicine cabinet. Quietly, the latches to Roger's heart shut from too much obligation, and my own heart closes from shame.

I keep finding dead birds splayed on the ground outside, next to the doors to the studio, the back of the house, and under the bedroom window. I am mad that a trick of the light confuses the birds into thinking there is no window glass and kills them instantly. I bury the birds by the creek and stack little river rocks over their hearts.

Roger and I decide to see a therapist. *He won't let you play any games*, a friend says. I want someone to drain my old blood and give me a transfusion. I want to know how we can survive chronic conditions. *You have to make a new boat*, my friend says.

But how do I find the strength?

Start fighting for each other, he replies. *Ask for help*. We schedule an appointment for the next week. The day of our first scheduled visit, our therapist dies of a heart attack, and we are on the ground in front of that door we never kicked open.

Roger's dreams circulate warmly through my bloodstream. I remember the years of how he wanted to live by the sea and paint beauty. But he no longer dreams, and my own lie quiet under a blanket of January snow. It's an apt metaphor for how I love this man: waiting for spring, for signs of life, praying that my blood still flows.

My blood is always hard to extract. *It's like getting blood from a stone*, the nurses complain. But the nice ones listen: like Susan at the Alpine Center who leans over my left arm and feels along the inside of my elbow. Her rubber gloves pat and slap. *Just trying to raise the veins*, she adds. I begin to instruct without instructing. *I'm not trying to tell you how to do your job. It's just that I have done this so many times. Use a butterfly needle.* I know about patience. I know about the hot pack nuked in the microwave lying across my arm, and the extra cups of water in tiny wax Dixie cups to get my blood moving. Other lab techs weigh in on the best site to hit a vein. I think blood and gold are the same: the same wishes to "hit" or "get" the vein and to make something of it. To send it to labs and melt it down, reduce it to get something real: for one, a white cell count; for the other, a ring.

I am blood type A. The book *Eat Right for Your Type* says that I am a descendent of the original vegetarians, fruits-and-grain-picking people. It tells me I should avoid all animal products, dairy, and wheat. It also states that type A people are more prone to cancer. I'm trying to figure out how my blood type knows what it likes to eat; how it smells out the cow and turns up its nose and instead reaches for the fresh plum from the tree; how it has become such a goody-goody.

I was raised a meat-and-potatoes girl in Ohio. I hated carrots, tomatoes, asparagus, and avocado. We ate rib-eye steak on Fridays and a leg of lamb on birthdays, Christmas Eve, and graduations. Did I eat too much mystery meat in boarding school? Too many turkey subs, burnt hamburgers, seared filets, and lamb chops in my "developing" years? Has my blood overdosed on protein: an acidic river boiling into my breast?

Of course, cancer theories don't fit on blackboards with underlined proofs at the bottom. Doctors always use both hands—maybe this, maybe that. What I do know is that my blood has turned on me. This beautiful highway of life, always moving in calculated measures in calculated directions, has pit stops and accelerations; but as long as it keeps coursing and checks in with my heart then all will be well. But something seems to have gone awry. The animals in my diet have gone wild, charging through my bloodstream, kicking their hooves against the sidewalls, shitting in all the wrong places. Meanwhile, little cancer cells are rallying their defenses, building little forts that grow into great castles.

I need to find out what blood type my children are.

. . .

Cameron pulls my elbow and draws me into the bathroom. *Mom, I started my period today*, she says, her eyes moist with excitement. We sit on the edge of the tub and talk. She was at basketball practice and found bloodstains on the white toilet paper in the locker room. My tears fall onto the top of my hands. *I knew you were going to cry*, Cameron says. She means, *I love you*. My bleeding happened for the first time in an outhouse at camp. My mother was a thousand miles away. I sat in the woods for most of the day, wondering whom to tell. When the camp counselor found me, she was angry that I had "disappeared" and told me there would be consequences. I couldn't look her in the eyes. Finally, I told her that I thought I had started my period. She gently took my hand and we walked to the infirmary to get some menstrual pads.

Brooke is born at home in a gush of blood. I hear a sound like a running faucet coming from near my feet. Once the bleeding stops, the midwives tell me that I need either to go to the hospital for a transfusion or stay in bed for a month. I decide on the latter. Brooke and I are meant for distances. For thirty days I move naked and pink across her tiny infinity, touching every part of her little body. Occasionally, there are interruptions: for a bowl of soup, a visit from a friend, for Taylor and Cameron to hold Brooke's tiny fingers. Some people say I am sacrificing too much. In a few hours I could have been made whole again with a transfusion. *But*, I say, *I want to make my own blood*.

Both Cameron and Brooke are conceived while I have my period. Dr. Julie tells me humans are like cats and that sometimes we drop an egg during intercourse. *Just like that.* There isn't much blood with Taylor. The doctor takes a thimbleful, to check if he has an infection. I remember a slick drop of blood on the cut end of the umbilical cord.

My mother never speaks about the blood, wetness, and pain of my own birth.

On a 747, Cameron and I are getting ready to go to sleep. I burrow into my seat like a marsupial, a dark blue fleece blanket tucked under my feet and pulled under my chin, a silk eye-pillow Velcroed behind my head, and my ears stuffed with plugs. I fall down the well of deep sleep and dream that a man sitting in the row in front of us is going to have a heart attack. Shocked, I wake up and tell Cameron about my dream. Three minutes later, the stewardess, in a controlled but clearly panicked voice, asks if there is a doctor on board the plane. Cameron turns to me and the blood drains from her face. I remember my mother's black eyebrows arching when I told her at eight years old that I dreamed our neighbor, Mrs. Wilhelm, died in a car accident. I saw her frozen look when I clambered down from the bus the next day and noticed an ambulance next door. But I don't have the heart for prophecy.

Three doctors are on the plane. Men rush with oxygen to the

seat two rows in front of us. The man's wife, wearing a tailored, black crepe suit, leans over her husband, unbuttoning his shirt. Cameron squeezes my forearm with her palm. They lay the man down and take his pulse, and a stewardess with a wet washcloth places it on his forehead. I hear one of the doctors say to the crying wife, *It's a mild heart attack.* The stewardess tells her she'll make arrangements for an ambulance to be present when we land.

Cameron's head falls on my shoulder. Her tears stain her white collar. Nothing needs to be said. She has spent years with my illness and long nights in her room with the music blaring. She has brought the perfunctory cups of tea to the side of my bed without a word. She remembers the silences in the car heading home after soccer practice. I think of what the heart has to do to avoid falling off the slippery edge into darkness, and how a twenty-one-year-old woman can crumble into an eight-year-old, her heart beating fast at night as she clutches her teddy bear.

In front of us, the old man lies asleep, peacefully. We can see how the back of his wife's head trembles, how we all carry on, as the plane races headlong into the night.

Dr. Charles takes me with him on his rounds to visit the HIV-positive children at the Mulago hospital in Kampala. As we pass through the large room of the adult ward, I see patients lying on black plastic mattresses; a lucky few have sheets. Each bed is angled; together they form a universe. Families are scattered on the floor, leaning against the walls or curled on their sides. Their eyes are glazed and they say nothing. I notice that under some of the beds are round metal pans filled with blood, sitting next to blood-soaked rags piled on the floor. I see trails of dark blood splats, and I shrink. I don't know what to do with this blood as it lives outside of the body: languid, dangerous, and cold.

I lean closer to Charles's shoulder, as if he could house me in his body and protect me from having to touch this blood. I picture the metal pans rattling as we pass and the people shaking them with outstretched arms. *Do something. Do something.* It's a chant that quickens my step and chases me down the narrowing hall. I imagine blood spilling all over the floor, seeping through the walls, babies screaming, and mothers with their cooking pots lying under their beds.

Charles introduces me to Elijah. He is six years old and has been HIV positive since birth. The child reaches his bone-thin arm, which has an IV attached to it with old, frayed, yellow tape, onto the top railing of his crib. His soft eyes are attempting to rally for the doctor with the stethoscope draped around his neck. The corners of his mouth lift into a faint smile. I want to touch Elijah's fingers and listen for the blood running through his veins and gather any blood that falls outside his body and put it back in again. If I could, I would take his face in my hands and say *Elijah, run. Run for your life.* I would meet him at the edge of the sea and see him leap into the waves, as he throws his body upward into the white foam.

And I would say the same to Roger and to myself: *Run for our lives. Let our blood flow.* No matter what distance, no matter what shape our relationship becomes, *leap.*

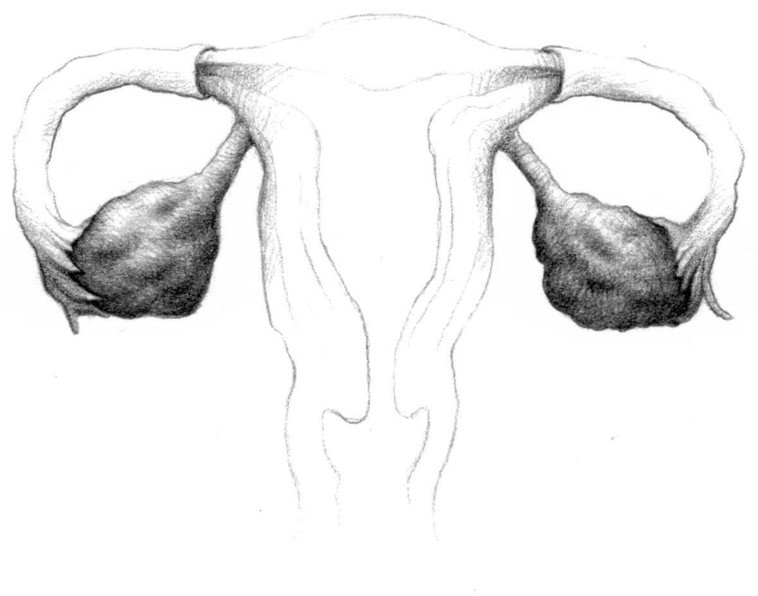

9

Ovaries

THE DIGITAL CLOCK on the bedside table reads four in the morning. Anxiety mounts the stairs and paces across the floor around my bed in his black patent-leather army boots, lecturing me about how I should take better care of myself. The sweat starts in my belly, travels along the back of my neck, and then pools behind my head. *You should have eaten more broccoli*, he pronounces. *You ought to get back to yoga class*. On and on he goes, intoning the usual litany of strategies to outsmart cancer. He turns his attention to the blood draw I am to have later that morning. *A test*, he notes. *Another test*. The genetic counselor says that it can take up to a month to get the results. What is at stake is the gene that tips the odds that I might get ovarian cancer. A rivulet of sweat lands in my belly button: the direction of fear. *How many have you taken* now? Anxiety asks. *How many have you failed?*

How many tests? My first one occurs in kindergarten. Mrs. Burgess, wearing an orange printed-cotton dress, leans on her elbow on the corner of my scratched wooden desk and tells us the consequences of cheating. *You little five-year-olds can learn right now how to be good little boys and girls*, she says. I curl my soft arms over the top of my head and tuck my chin down as if I'm already guilty. Cynny wriggles next to me, her feet swinging like a pendulum as though she's trying to get enough momentum to gain liftoff and rocket away from the spelling test. C-A-T. D-O-G. R-U-N.

The directions for the Scholastic Aptitude Test (the SAT) are impossible. It lasts three hours and forty-five minutes, and in three sections it will test me in math and critical reading. Each question is a multiple choice with five answers. It feels as though yellow number two pencils are torturing me, and even an eraser can't rub out the leaden evidence that I'm not as smart as my brother Deke. I can't compete with his almost-perfect scores, his science experiments in the basement, or the vials full of sulfur hanging in wood slots nailed to the wall.

I decide to be tough instead. I've got so much determination and thrust that my right arm shakes. I fill in the circles with an enthusiasm that spikes when I know the answer. When I have to make a choice between two or even three answers, my chest deflates and I'm driven into the front of my head. Trying to outsmart the smart, I take a stab in the dark. By the time I reach the math section the air has gone completely out of my lungs. I rub the back of my neck. In thirty minutes, I realize that I won't be going to Yale. I watch the ash tree rustling outside the window where the test is taking place, and notice the way the auburn hair of the girl in front of me falls down her back.

Less than a decade later, I'm sitting on the toilet, huddled over the paper strip, trying to line it up with the colors on the package. *This test is easy*, they say. *One you can take at home*. What they don't tell you is that you have to balance the package on your knee and that it's an art not to pee all over your hand and hold the strip so you don't drop it down the toilet. I take a total of three of these tests in eight years and pass each one. Each little bit of pee shudders forth a miracle, the fuchsia color blushing so strongly all over the paper that I become shy. Taylor, Cameron, and Brooke stirring inside of me turn my pee into a painting.

For Taylor, I wait on the toilet for what seems an age, allowing my future to arrive slowly. For Cameron, I run out of the bathroom with the paper still in my hand and find Taylor in the greenhouse racing his blue plastic car. I show him the pink strip and tell him that he's going to have a baby brother or sister: a friend, *someone to play with*. Taylor holds the paper in his hand up to the window, as if he could take that paper in his arms. For Brooke, like Cameron, the test is the miracle of conceiving during my period. I am astonished by the smell of roses that comes from my body, the aroma of my child. I sit on the bathroom floor and follow the layers of shock through my body. I feel the counterclockwise turning in my belly, a tingling, almost itching sensation sliding down my arms. A glaze thickens inside my head. Taylor and Cameron bang on the bathroom door. *Mommy*, they shout. *What are you doing in there?*

I refuse to answer Anxiety. A nurse named Betty, who wears a pale yellow-and-rose floral jacket instead of the conventional medical mint green, injects the one lousy vein I have on my left arm with a red liquid. *This is the dye that will light up your bones*, she says. My hackles rise. *What is this?* I ask myself. *Am I a Christmas tree with lights made of cancer?* I roll over, waiting the required time for the dye to "take" while I slide down the hole of fear. What if I don't pass *this* test? I've heard that if you pass the other tests—the brain scan, the chest x-ray, the liver enzymes—and you fail this one, that bone cancer will take a long time to kill you. On the other hand, if you fail two tests you can expect an early death. This is a final exam. *How can one test have so much weight?* I think. *How can sheer plastic film be so heavy?* I feel as if a chunk of iron ore is lodged in my heart. Painful, this business in the bones. The human skeleton is 20 percent of our total body weight, which means that my bones weigh twenty-six pounds. That is greater than the weight of my three babies at birth, more than my carry-on suitcase. More than I can handle.

Days later, when the pathologist has graded his papers, I'm told that I passed. I immediately think of those women who've failed. No one is at the head of the class. There's no way to prepare or buy Cliff Notes. There are no older students around to coach you. Who are the women who get an *F*? Are they the ones looking at pictures in the oncologist's office, sitting in leather chairs discussing the black smears on the film of their bones? What do they think of the skeletons hanging from the light box like a bad etching? And the oncologist waving his index finger at the shadows? Passing this kind of test is like crawling on my hands and knees through a low wooden door, my back barely brushing the grain.

What does BRCA stand for? I ask. The doctor explains: (BR) east (CA)ncer. BRCA1 and 2. The mutation is located on the long arm of chromosome 13q12 positioned at 12.3. Positive men and women don't have the protein needed to fight tumor formation. A simple blood draw indicates whether you have the mutation or not. This time, there is no multiple choice; you either pass or fail.

My doctor asks me why I waited so long to get the test. I tell him that my father took the test only recently, and failed, as did either *his* father or mother, or their parents and grandparents. As I look at the chart, I wonder how I will tell my children that if I have the mutation they have a 50 percent chance of carrying it, too. This is the first test I'm taking for someone else; and it's not just for anyone else, but for my own children.

I want to fail. The stakes are so high I'm already exhausted, an ocean swimmer trying to cut through whitecaps. What was once an idea, a high-minded concept, comes to me for the first time as knowledge in flesh and blood: I will give my own life for my children. I feel as though I'm already lifting the car off their bodies, with one arm. Who can carry the weight of words like *positive* or *diagnosis*? And what about their future children, my grandchildren, looking through the window of the surgery, while the body parts of their mothers are hacked off, blood clotting on the floor?

I drive alone to the office on the third floor, the one on the right just past the oncology clinic. I have never gone this far down the corridor. The chrome plaque says *genetic counselor*. *This is the protocol*, the doctor explains. *You have to see the counselor. You have to be sure you know what you are taking.* He looks sternly at me. *Consequences*, he adds, *are forever*, as if I wasn't already aware of that.

Penelope, a young woman with a long black braid, is to be my counselor. She has made a career of telling women the good and the bad news and of weighing the choices. "Good" news means that you have the same odds as any woman of getting breast cancer. "Bad" news means that you have a 40 to 60 percent chance of getting breast cancer and a 20 to 30 percent chance of ovarian cancer. Penelope says that if it is bad news I might want to consider an oophorectomy.

Could you pronounce that again? I ask.

Actually, she says, *it's a bilateral salpingo-oophorectomy. It means the surgical removal of both ovaries and fallopian tubes.*

I read the material in the pamphlet while Penelope slips out for a coffee refill:

> *Genetic counselors are health professionals with specialized graduate degrees and experience in the areas of medical genetics and counsel-*

ing. They identify families at risk, investigate the problem present in the family, interpret information about the disorder, analyze inheritance patterns and risks of recurrence, and review available options with the family.

I check out the picture on the wall of Penelope and two female friends (sisters, perhaps?) in an inflatable raft, paddling through very big rapids. It makes sense a woman of adventure would choose this job, guiding women through the emotional and medical rapids. Penelope tells me that it would be a shock if I wasn't positive since my father tested positive and I'd had breast cancer already.

So young, she says.

I know.

Penelope and I sign a form that ensures I understand what I am choosing. Strangely coupled though I am with her, I feel alone. It's as if I'm going spelunking. I can sense how dark the cave is, and how narrow. I already know that I have to crawl in by myself and that the way out is through. Penelope takes my hand in hers. *Good luck.* She smiles. I don't know whether to lower my head and duck out of the room or take this intimacy to mean something. I look up and notice that there are mica-colored streaks in her irises. I walk back down the corridor into the lab I know so well. It takes a long time to draw four vials from me.

Penelope won't inform me over the phone. I feel like I'm being told I have to go to class to get my grade. *Well, no surprise,* she says, placing her sporty glasses on her lap. *You're positive.*

I try to maintain my balance on the thin line between suspicion and diagnosis. On the outside, I'm casual; on the inside, I'm falling over. I fix my eyes on the diploma on the wall with a degree in something I've never heard of. The gold seal looks like a sunburst, the calligraphy signature as standard as the routine she now begins. My heart races in time with Penelope's voice running across the page of options. I drift in and out of her voice, my weight forward in the chair—as if I can take it.

Half to my surprise, I find I can: for this moment is yet another bead on my string of illnesses and remembrances. *You can do this*, says Dr. Brenton. *Half my patients have success*, reports Dr. Thompson. *The good news is you only have two lymph nodes involved*, remarks Dr. Sitarik. *This is where we will make the incision*, informs Dr. Gjos, his pen drawing lines on my breasts. I remember how it goes: how I nod as I listen and ask questions that are brave.

But my gut rumbles and rants. *I am sick of this body-care business. I haul it around every day; shower it; put crème on it; comb its hair, put underwear on it, then pants, bra, and shirt; walk it (with the dog); put it in the car; place it on a chair in front of the computer; stand it in front of the kitchen sink to do the dishes; get it comfortable on the couch to read the newspaper; put food in it—I mean lots of food, strawberries and bananas and grilled eggplant and sausage; burp it, walk it again, stretch it, do yoga for it; undress it, fluff pillows for it, and put it in bed. Exhausting. Boring. I need to buy a trailer for it, haul it to the ocean, slide it into the water, and let it dissolve back into its source. Or maybe I need to buy a chariot, the winged kind, and fly it to the sun. Push it off its seat, watch it melt back into light. No one warned me this body-hauling business was going to get so tiring. God I need to break free. Unburden myself. Walk off the job.*

Penelope reviews my options again. We stare at the neat, colored charts with graphs correlating the percentages of breast and ovarian cancer risk and age compared to the average woman's chances. I'm being told I'm not average. Only 5 to 10 percent of women who get breast cancer have this gene.

I wonder what women thought before the discovery of genetic history. What did they think when they watched their grandmothers and then mothers lying upstairs behind hushed doors, dying of cancer at early ages? They would have seen doctors coming into the house late at night, in the middle of a snowstorm, carrying black leather bags. But no one sat in an office, legs crossed at the ankles, and explained the odds to the children using charts and supplying them with cups of hot coffee. No genetic counselor reached for their hands and told them they would follow their family *like a hawk*, that they'd call them once a year to check up, that they'd be rooting for them.

Penelope closes the blue folder with my name on a white strip at the bottom. *Any more questions?* she asks.

Just one, I think. *How exactly do I tell my children?*

I don't know how to relate to the idea of carrying a gene. Does it mean I'm carrying a suitcase or a bomb? Or a bomb in a suitcase? I mentally scan the inside of my body to see where the gene was left: under the stairwell of my rib cage? Behind my delicate wrists? I wonder how I could have carried something my whole life and not known about it. No airport security has asked me whether this particular suitcase has been in my possession the whole time. Now it has a name: BRCA2.

The doctor tells me that it would be best if I have my ovaries removed. *It's not a big deal,* he states. *Just two inch-long scars on each side of your abdomen above your ovaries. Another one just above the bikini line. And, of course, another scar in your belly button where the camera is inserted. That should unpack the suitcase and dismantle the bomb permanently.*

I stare out the window, from which a foot-long icicle is melting. I cannot help but think of the impermanence of my own body, its round, female parts melting away.

I want to tell the genetic counselor, nurses, and doctors that, in addition to BRCA2, my father packed love inside my suitcase too. He laid out things like trust, a passion for boats, and a twinkle in the eye—the last of which Taylor shares. He stuffed in toleration and generosity, tenderness, and delight in bird feeders and rowing at night. And, when the suitcase couldn't get any fuller, he slipped in Cameron's new ideas about fairness and Brooke's love of dogs. I wonder if he ever knew how much I love my own body.

My friend Priya gently suggests that I don't need my ovaries—*anymore*. I know she is telling me that it is time to say goodbye to the mother in me, the eternal caretaker; that my ovaries are no longer the pearls strung for other people's necks; that they have served their purpose. Strangely, I start to notice twins, and everywhere mothers walking down the mall with strollers so big they look like mini-cars. Two babies are perched, one in front of the other, their little hands gripping the front rail. I stare right through these mothers' abdomens and bless their ovaries for doing such a good job: the double miracle of twin eggs and twin babies.

My father's father had an identical twin. My great-grandmother had an egg that divided in two and produced Ed and Don, who looked so much alike that they could even fool their grade-school teachers. My grandmother tells me that when they were boys, Ed took a swatting on his bare butt for Don in exchange for a candy bar. No one knew the difference. Ed was the first to die. Don got Alzheimer's and began to wander the streets late at night. On one occasion, Don's wife found him asleep on Ed's grave.

The doctor says I need an ultrasound of my ovaries before surgery, *just to check that they aren't enlarged.* The technician named Cindy takes me back to the inner chamber, away from the aging man playing the piano in the lobby of the hospital to dissipate any notion it's a scary place. The hospital administration wants us to feel like we're sitting on couches in our living rooms. I follow Cindy down a long hallway. She is young, with smooth skin, and she clutches a clipboard to her large breasts while she chats about how cold it is, and how the temperature gauge in her car read one degree at seven this morning on her way to work. *This is my first winter in Boulder. Everyone says it's been the coldest on record,* she says. *Global warming,* she clucks. Cindy points to the changing room and the lockers. *Take everything off. Did you drink plenty of water?*

I enjoy this part, making some joke about how we should hurry since I might dribble over the floor. *Old age,* I warn, *you know how the bladder goes.*

We giggle like two school-aged girls in on something together. We need a moment to break the ice before Cindy inserts a lubricated probe high into my vagina. *First, we'll squeeze warm gel across your pubis and look for your ovaries from above*, she says, as though the probe is some kind of Hubble telescope taking a snapshot of two moons orbiting my abdomen. She slides the egglike object first across the right side, then the left, ironing the creases on my skin. Cindy points to the TV monitor: *That little sack, shaded in grainy black, is your uterus*. I look up and imagine my children as fetuses, their little hearts pumping. I'd like to believe they are all there still, on TV, swimming away. How did Taylor (all six feet of him) fold himself up so small? I feel the shock of love's first home.

Cindy can't seem to find either ovary. *Sometimes they drift away after pregnancy, go into hiding*, she explains. *They're the size of almonds*. She tries again, pushing hard on my belly with her left hand as she searches across my pubic bone. Nothing. She has me roll my pelvis farther to the left: still nothing. I move farther to the right: yet again, nothing.

OK, let's try looking from the inside, Cindy suggests. I get to insert the slippery wand inside myself. We make the customary fuss over paper drapes, and eyes are averted. I appreciate the gesture, but I am *so* over modesty at this point in my health career. We still can't find my ovaries, even from inside. Cindy pushes the probe in further, and then pulls it until it is virtually out of my body. She chitchats over the fact that this borders on something sexual.

I'm beginning to wonder if Cindy is inept or if my ovaries are just pulling the great escape. Cindy explains that it is unusual not to find them on the internal exam, but that it happens sometimes. On the monitor, my bladder looks like a bulging balloon changing shape every time Cindy makes a deeper pass. Now it has become a starfish floating out to sea.

Oh, well, Cindy sighs. *We sure did try. Go ahead and pee, get dressed, and we'll talk about next steps.* On the toilet I think about how typical this situation is. I'm always the "special" patient. Cindy can't find my ovaries. They're like children running away from home, hiding out in the neighbor's toolshed, and wanting to come home for dinner when they're ready. I imagine they're sick of being told what to do. Cindy tells me that the images look clear and that my doctor will call to see if I need to have a CAT scan or an MRI. *Christ*, I think. *Another test.* As I walk to the car I squeeze my eyes. Snow is falling against the shrouded shape of the Flatirons. It looks like an ultrasound of a Colorado landscape.

My Japanese friend tells me about the ultimate delicacy he finds in a famous fish market in Tokyo: the ovary of the octopus; *takomanma* in Japanese. The night after my ultrasound, I dream that I reach for a jar of blueberry jam in the cupboard. Instead of grabbing blueberry, I grab a quart jar with two white-and-yellow swirled marbles suspended in oil. I have found my ovaries.

Kathryn and I sit on the hot rocks on Dawson Island for a picnic on a late afternoon in July. We meet each other once a year in Canada, flying by each other on the lake in our outboard boats stacked with children. We carry the same language, the loss of body parts and fear of dying. Kathryn's athletic arms swirl when she tells me that having her ovaries removed was like the last movement, the finale to her ordeal. She'd had a mastectomy, reconstruction, chemotherapy, radiation, and a nipple graph. But the doctors were concerned that her estrogen production was too high, too female. They told her it was time for an oophorectomy as though it was time for bed.

Kathryn tells me the operation is minor compared to everything else, like a small aftershock after the earthquake; the high, thin clouds after the explosion. I look at the way her eyes shine with feminine pride and how her light brown hair has grown back curlier around the nape of her neck. I start to think about relative suffering, in both senses of the word. How bad could an oophorectomy be for Kathryn after the loss of her brother from AIDS? My losses, those small piles of my own flesh, pale in comparison to others. I tell myself that this next surgery can't be that bad. It's a P.S., a postscript. This is what it means to have elective surgery.

My skin will be broken into and my ovaries sucked out. The insides of my eggs will ooze down the sides of a stainless-steel medical extractor. I will wear a white cotton gown opened in the front with a white blanket heated to keep me from shaking. In fact, the last thing I will see before I sleep will be the white walls of the surgery room and the white masks over the nurses' faces. Whiteness will fill me, spreading down my tracheal tube into the back of my throat and my eyelids. It will spread from the lining of my stomach like a mist, flowing down the inside channels of my arms and legs, from the top of my uterus down my fallopian tubes to my ovaries. Eventually, whiteness will seep through the pores of my skin and fill the space around my body until I rest inside a huge white home, where it is quiet. There, I hope I can be made whole again.

I decide to wait until June, when the weather will be warm, to have my ovaries removed. I want to have fertility around me: the yellow pollen flying, the honeybees sucking the hearts from flowers and spreading their sugary secrets. I want the azaleas, rhododendrons, irises, and lilies multiplying in my garden. While I recover, I can watch the red rosebush bloom on the trellis and see the hummingbirds sink their long beaks into their petaled skirts before their beating wings back up with a flourish and they enter the next rose. I want to watch all this sex from my bed.

I make my pilgrimage again to the ocean. It is ritual I always take before surgery—a kind of baptism, as I am welcomed into the nurturing waters. I pack my earplugs, snorkel, and fins. I take with me the picture of the kids with their arms around each other. I want to take out each organ of my body and wash it in the saltwater: to cleanse my liver of fear, my heart of grief, my kidneys of failures, my intestines of the unacceptable, my stomach of disbelief, my appendix of outrage, my spleen of exhaustion, my pancreas of inertia.

When the last grain of salt has been washed off, I'll put them back in their places, as though I'm stocking the pantry. I'll store each organ where it belongs, prepared for another year: fresh, sealed inside the juices of my body. The bladder will be on the first shelf, then kidneys and intestines, stomach, spleen, and pancreas. The second shelf will stock the liver, esophagus, and lungs. The heart will occupy the entirety of the third shelf.

I don't bother with the female organs. In a few weeks, my ovaries will be tossed up on the beach, like bleached nautilus shells. I fantasize that some little girl with a ponytail and a tiny bikini will collect them in her turquoise beach bucket. She will take them home along with the other shells and place them on her bedside table and store them together, inseparable. I hope she keeps them her entire life and tells her daughter the story of how she was on vacation with her parents, how the shells glowed in the dark—like moonlight, like little lamp oracles—and contained a miracle.

I come home renewed. The ocean moves inside of me, washing up and down my legs. The full moon rises in my belly, and my uterus is lined with shiny wet sand.

The night before my operation I check my list. Do I have my slippers in my overnight bag? Have the plants in the living room been watered? I'm not afraid. My body has learned trust over the years. I am becoming a great tree. Deep within me, I know about winter and how sap moves in thick channels, how I can't bloom without the cold, dark nights. The slightest stirring reminds me that the next season will come and this body will rise again off the surgery table.

That night I dream of a chipped wooden boat tiller in my hand. It's a perfect fit, and my fingertips circle its firm waist and feel the wood's rough, sun-bleached strength. Strangely, the tiller isn't attached to a rudder, hull, mast, sail, or anything that belongs to a ship. Yet my feet are placed on something solid, like wood. I have the sensation of water gently rising and falling underneath me, an ancient, ceaseless rocking that has never left me, even in the worst of times.

I remember one August when my father and I were in a sailboat race. A blackening squall raced down the channel from the Northwest, and my father's knuckles held on to the tiller so tightly that they turned ashen white. I lost the mainsheet line and my father screamed over the wind for me to reach out and grab hold of it. My thin, adolescent body shook from the cold and the terror. But I couldn't move. My father yelled for me to take the tiller, which was now fighting to be free of any control, and stretched his six-foot-three-inch body out so far I was convinced he was going to fall overboard. But he didn't, and I was left with the tiller frozen in my hand.

The morning of the operation is warm and clear, the sky brightening over the plains. When Thomas and Priya arrive, I am calm. I wipe down the kitchen counters, sit on the couch, and check to see if I put some almonds in my purse. I walk into the garden. I stroke my dog's smooth black ears back toward his neck.

We turn onto Foothills Highway and the past and future slide into a moment. As we aim the car into the hospital parking lot, time chases me toward the thin aluminum handle of the hospital door. The hallways, forms to fill in, paper shoes, and the tiny, draped sterile room are so routine that I feel like I am on an endless escalator. My mouth tastes like paper, and my stomach growls from the lack of food and water. I sense a wounded quality to the nurse's voice and I wonder what could have caused such sorrow. I try to cheer her up by being casual, showing her where the good vein might be hiding. She manages a smile. When I smile.

I remember my dream and think of how weightless and adrift I feel on this empty sea. My trusty tiller points toward the surgery room door, through which I will sail to disappear over the horizon of anesthesia. My boat will sink and I will be abandoned to a self that no longer dreams or sleeps or tosses or turns. My skin will turn a pasty white and my eyes will bulge behind my pale, veined lids. Fish will cruise by the wreck.

I wake up from the operation, shaking. My body is pinned to the bed, just like the children with malaria I saw in Uganda, who were curled so tight against the wall, whose thin bodies I'd tried to unfold, my hand rubbing their bony spines. A nurse speaks to me through the fog, telling me that she's going to give me a shot of Demerol to calm the shakes. I try to turn my head to the right as if to place myself back inside my body, rotate my chin to span the distance from my death sleep to this nurse pointing a needle at my arm. The nurse smiles vaguely and I slide back down the ravine.

I hear crying from somewhere and the metal side of the bed pushing against me. I am dreaming a memory of a little Ugandan boy asking his mother for more water, how his lips were swollen and dotted with white pus. His mother leaned against his hospital bed and accidentally kicked the cooking stove underneath. She was so tired she barely raised her chin off the railing. I reached for the paper cup of water and handed it to her. She lifted herself and brought the cup to his lips and the water dribbled over the corners of his mouth. The nurse tries to make me eat a cracker with a sip of water from a paper cup so I can take a pain pill. This way, I won't have to spend the night in the hospital, shaking.

My mind searches through the vast, empty space where my ovaries once lived. The wind blows through this landscape on its way south, and yet it is strangely peaceful, as if a question is being asked of me: *What will take their place?* I want to say things like *classical music*, *painting*, but I know that I shouldn't answer, at least not yet. I lie in bed and look out through the French doors. The grass is pushing up to its full height and the cottonwood is in leaf. Summer is radiating through the west window across my sheet and I watch the creases fill with darkness. The world is within reach.

I dream:

> The surgeon is taking my ovaries. He lifts them gently upwards. I begin to say the two million blessings for the number of immature eggs that I brought into this world as a newborn baby girl. I bless my mother and her two million eggs and my grandmother and her eggs and her mother and her mother. I bless all women who can't have children. I bless my sister-in-law for the hard work of trying to have her own babies. And choosing to adopt.

> I bless Leila and Katherine and Nancy and Mahabba for the loss of their ovaries. For the violence of rupture. For their bravery. The two million names of God. The surgeon smiles and says that because I know the two million blessings he wants me to know a secret. Something he has seen in other surgeries. He tells me there is a small window of time, right after he takes them out, that something can descend and take their places. Especially when the woman knows the two million blessings. I sit up and watch two columns of swirling golden light enter my pelvis. He asks, *Do you know what this is?* He says, *This is pure creation.*

I don't know how to believe that I can't have children anymore. It's like being told that the sun won't rise tomorrow. I pat the little scars on my belly. *Barren*, I say to myself. In my mind, I visit the remote tundras of the planet and walk for days across their cold winter surfaces. I create poems of fertility in my head—of foliage and petals of fire, of a child's laughter down the hall, and of the way the crescent moon faithfully returns to its fullness. Two million fertile words dash this way and that over the page.

I read that the female brain changes dramatically after menopause and completely after her ovaries are removed. Estrogen and progesterone and oxytocin stop boosting the communication and emotional circuits that drive a woman to tend for others at all costs. The brain that once marinated in feel-good neurohormones during pregnancy is no longer.

My brain is letting go. The margins of my mother and father and my brothers and my children's bodies are disappearing.

A new woman sits here at my desk. The little-girl brain, the adolescent brain, the wife brain, the mommy brain have passed away. I now live with the on-my-own brain, with its own cycling of fear and joy, keeping me company in my breakfast nook, at my writing desk, and on my afternoon walks. It asks me to put words down, to watch them branch and bloom.

This new brain stacked somewhere inside my skull has, however, traveled all this way with me, and has committed to go the whole distance. I rest inside an order I cannot comprehend. Though my brain, like my father's, could unloosen at any time, I strangely have little fear. I've learned that the future tense has its own destiny. It is a wild force, larger than me. For now, I can see the cottonwoods outside my office in their winter. I know that spring will come soon enough. I think about their lives: who gave birth to whom, who is taller, and who leafs out farther. I bear witness, as if they could say, *We have seen hard winters and soggy springs, fiery summers and gorgeous autumns. We rise and fall, each season becoming us.* I, too, have known the passing of years. Next year, winter might be easy, spring dry, summer thundery, and autumn passing quickly for both of us. We share in uncertain seasons.

The truth is that I have no more thoughts about my ovaries. Their place in my body has simply drifted away. The story is over and the back cover closed. I don't want them back and don't wonder where they went or what they're up to. I don't think if I'm more or less whole from their death. My scars just lie on the surface like little ribbons, rather than tunnels leading to dry cisterns. I don't know how it is that absence silently fills with something else. But it does, like the way the snow wraps itself over the quince tree.

I feel oddly at peace. Any identity I might have had as a "sick person" or a "patient" has worn itself out. My mind is learning to let things be, just as they are. The accumulation of loss has no more room. My breasts have floated away, parts of my ear, bone in my skull, moles, tonsils, lymph nodes, hair, blood, ovaries, fallopian tubes, breasts are all frothing and foaming in the waves, then vanishing from sight. I watch from a new place, somewhere beyond my skin—a place I can only say is located everywhere, in the water and the wave and the stars and the black ink of night, but at the same time, nowhere.

The elephants are restless. Eight adults and two infants are standing in a line with their rear left feet shackled in thick iron chains. Baby Abu paws the dry African ground. *He's the troublemaker,* a trainer exclaims. Everyone smiles. The mahouts, the notorious elephant trainers, tell our small group the rules:

1. Never step directly in front of the elephants.
2. Ask for help to climb up into the saddle.
3. Feed the elephants only vegetable treats.

I reach for Brooke's hand. Our dream is happening. We are about to ride elephants for five days through the African bush and the floodwaters of the Okavango Delta, Botswana. Our elephants are highly trained. They have been rescued from circuses in the

United States and reintroduced to their home in Africa. Brooke turns to me. *Thank you,* she says, as if she already knows.

The mahout gives the command for *down* and Cathy, one of the mother elephants, drops very slowly to her front knees, then lowers her backside to the ground. I lower my head as I approach. All I have in my sight are eyes and tusks and leather-gray skin. The climb up her side is easy. I swing my legs into the rectangular box that is cinched with long padded straps around her belly. Cathy rises from the ground as gracefully as anything I have ever known.

Cathy is a new mother. Her baby girl, only two months old, is standing just above Cathy's ankles. She walks right next to her as we move out of camp and begin to wade through the clear waters. Her movements are steady, each foot placed solidly, and ponderously, yet as fluid as the pools below. When we reach the other side, Cathy shreds a huge branch of an acacia tree of its leaves in minutes. She munches and crunches, and then sounds a low guttural blast that vibrates through my calves, all the way into my pelvis, and rolls through my cells. My own throat gasps with a sound I've never heard.

I am sitting close to Cathy's wrinkled forehead and the rim of her flapping ears. The "fingers" at the end of her trunk search for treats from the mahout sitting in front of me. I am close to the giraffes floating through the bush across the waterway and to the elephants in front of me, elongating their trunks toward the scent of zebra. The African landscape spreads out before me, a horizon lined in charcoal shot through with rays of yellow. Before us are small clumps of grass and, in the distance, a plain spreads out, dotted with acacia thickets. The first lavender wisp of cloud is forming in the east.

It seems like bliss to have nowhere to go. I drink water from the bottle nestled in the saddle behind me and scan for lions. I watch the wonder that shapes Brooke's raised eyebrows as she rides her elephant. My legs drape over Cathy's massive sides, and my hands entwine themselves in silence as heat wets my hair at the nape.

I look down at Cathy's long, wiry eyelashes. I remember my dream only months before of a medicine man offering me the eyelash of an elephant. *One eyelash can not only save you,* he said. *It can save the world.* Everywhere I turn, I feel saved. The smell of dried grass and the sway of the elephant beneath me are saving me. Cathy's eyelash is saving me. Her thick legs, her uterus still stretched from birth, her nipples engorged with milk, her ears, trunk, tusks, belly, feet, skin, tail, hair, and ovaries. She is complete. When we enter the waters again, Cathy lifts her newborn with her trunk. She is carrying her child as she carries me. A new fertility finds me.

The world as I've known it is far away, dwarfed by the scale of elephant and my own heart cracked open by Cathy and her child. Beneath us is Africa and the elephants who have moved across its surface, those who in the millennia have marked the ancient pathways with their tread. Each step, carefully placed, has left its weight behind—kicking up fine dust that plumes briefly and is then sifted into the dry air.

. . .

Cameron and I are like Russian wooden dolls, one nested inside another. When she was born, her tiny ovaries were already filled with thousands of eggs, my grandchildren spinning inside of her. When she prepared to get married, I thought of how her child's little feet were already reaching for her shoreline.

Soon enough, her baby is ready. I raise Cameron's hand when her eyes go pale from the pain. *You can do this*, I say. The baby crowns, wet flecks of brown hair and pink skin, and the room floods with morning light. I place one hand in Cameron's, the other hand in Brooke's, and a current flows between a mother, her daughters, and a granddaughter. As Cameron lifts her baby and places her on her breast, our tears flow over Isabella's tiny face. Ten fingers, we count. Ten toes. Two million eggs.

In Crestone, Colorado, the aspen leaves have turned gold. As I hike in the foothills of the Sangre De Cristo Mountains, I find a tiny Hindu temple. Inside, standing in the center on a dais, is a six-foot-tall marble statue of a Hindu goddess shipped from India. A young devotee lives in a one-room cabin nearby and bathes and dresses the statue. Every day, for six years, the goddess has worn a freshly ironed sari: pink for Monday, saffron for Tuesday, and so on. The devotee lays fresh fruit, jasmine rice, and a bowl of floating white mums at her feet.

When I enter, I duck as if to bow. The goddess has small features; her jet-black eyes are lined in kohl, and her fingers are so thin they could break. The sun slants through the circular window from the west, ruthlessly hot. I sit on a purple silk cushion in front of the goddess and study her neck, translucent and white, for signs of sweat.

I want to believe.

The goddess stares ahead, as if she's intent on seeing through something. I turn around to look at her line of sight only to realize that I am the subject of her focus. Embarrassed, I shut my eyes. Suddenly a perfectly formed vision arises, like a cloud emerging above the mountain. An orange liquid is pouring from every orifice in her body—from her mouth, ears, tear ducts, vagina, and the tiny slits in her hands and feet. I see the entire world below her with billions of people scurrying this way and that, busy being human. Hunched over and full of purpose, do they realize that a gorgeous golden nectar is being poured over their backs onto the ground? Is it only a few bright, knowing ones who have tilted their heads upward to drink from the source of all life?

I feel my chin being raised and my lips lightly parted. I taste the sweet sensation of pure orange-blossom juice gliding down my throat. Then she says: *Don't take your suffering so personally.* A jolt of grief breaks open my chest. The weight of loneliness lifts out of its cage and my eyes tear with a relief I haven't felt in years. Everything is released in the proportion of her generosity. Thankful, I bow, hands clasped together. *It's not personal, Ginny,* I tell myself. *It's not personal at all.*

I'd like to believe that the goddess smiled at me then; that she stepped down from her pedestal and walked with me in the cool mountain air; that we exchanged gifts, my pearl-drop earrings for a few more words that I could take with me and turn over like a smooth stone in my pocket. I'd like to believe she told me her name.

On leaving, I take one last look. I notice her little closet of clothes, her delicate porcelain feet with a ring painted gold on her baby toe, the flies circling the wedges of pineapple. When I take her eyes into mine, she is beyond this world.

Millie is cooking breakfast. She scoops the crushed Katogo into seven plastic bowls, four for her own children, and three for those of her dead friend. We laugh: the baby won't let go of my fingers. Beads of sweat roll off the back of her neck. Next door, a sister sings to her baby as the sun heads to its blazing zenith. Millie leans over the cooking pot and slowly takes off the metal top. *There is an old African saying*, she says. *Lift the lid of your pot slowly to let the steam out of your suffering*. She tells me that three of her seven children have died of AIDS. *All the women here in the camp have lost children*, she adds. She is as matter-of-fact as the taut clothesline that stretches across the opening of her hut. A terrified stillness descends on me. I am determined to remain, and stand my ground, as if I could place myself on the landscape of her loss.

How do you do it? I ask Millie. *How do you carry on?*

She looks me in the eye. *My women sisters' arms are long enough to hold my sorrow. No one is left alone. No one owns their suffering.*

EPILOGUE

IT IS THE EVENING OF JULY 4TH, 2011. I am babysitting my granddaughter Isabella while her parents have a last night out before their second child arrives. I am slumped on their couch in the TV room, the windows wide open and a fan on at full speed. There is a drought in New Mexico and now fires in Los Alamos have filled the air with smoke for miles. I have felt hot all day and my eyes sting from the ash.

I hear the booms and cracks of the fireworks and look out of the window for the colored sparkles in the sky. I turn off all the lights and sit and think about other Fourth of Julys, especially the nights on the Maumee River, floating on a barge with my mother, father, and brothers, and piles of other kids and parents. I remember the huge white-and-red flower shapes blooming overhead and reflecting on the water's surface. I never wanted it to end.

At this stage of life I can pass on all the big revelry. Celebrations for me now are very small and private—like the warm feeling of the dark, or the safety of being twenty miles away from the fire. I think of how I love this little girl, asleep in her crib, unaware of this day of independence. My head throbs and I get up for a glass of water, watching how I have developed the practice of turning the dial down on my complaints and carrying on anyway.

I still manage symptoms: chronic ear-ringing, headaches, neck pain, low-grade vertigo, deep fatigue. Some days they are strong enough to throw me back to bed. On those days, I navigate the ancient tides of hope and fear. Some doctors tell me that the symptoms are the byproducts of chemotherapy and surgeries; others say I'm lucky to be alive. I know this. In every cell of my body, I know this. I don't take for granted even the simplest movement of turning on the faucet to fill my glass. When gravity is my friend, I give thanks.

Yet I've never felt so vital. I love how my body moves. I strangely feel more like a woman than ever before. My sexuality lives all the way though me. I believe this has something to do with the sheer fact that life required I either get farther into my body or get out. There is not so much in-between now. I don't want to pick at the small things or be mean to my body by not liking my stomach roll or the size of my upper arms. I look at other people's bodies differently. I realize, especially in our "midlife" bodies, that we're all losing parts. Gravity takes over and bellies start to sag; cheeks droop and chins double; hair grays and jowls develop. When I look at photos of me in my twenties, I smile at the innocence radiating from my eyes. I had no idea what was in store.

I wander through Cameron and Adam's house, looking at the silver picture frames that house family photos: of Taylor, his wife Nicole, and Brooke. I scan the distances to where they are tonight and wonder if they're celebrating in a stadium or staying at home. I think how hardwired this tendency is for a mother: always tracking her children's comings and goings. I've become fluid in my own comings and goings, as if each step I make is both empty and full of purpose.

The house is now quiet, the fireworks finale over. There is an order to this moment: as if its small size is compressed into a kind of greatness. This is what it means to carry on, to take the next step. I place my foot forward and stand in the center of the kitchen. I sense how Isabella's little feet have toddled back and forth on the brick floor; how soon her little sister will be next to her; and how much I want to live for a very long time.

—July 4th, 2011

ACKNOWLEDGMENTS

TO MY PARENTS, David and Georgia Welles, and my four brothers, Deke, Jeff, Peter, and Chris: thank you for teaching me the power and necessity of family and home. Thank you for the hundreds of football games in the backyard, the kindnesses that can only come from family. You rooted for me. Even at a physical distance, you were my champions, always affirming that I could walk the path I was given, make the hard choices, and no matter what the outcome, emerge stronger.

To all my dearest friends (each of you knows who you are): I am on my knees in gratitude. You drove me to doctors' appointments. You cooked my favorite meals—baked potatoes with sour cream and strawberry and rhubarb pie—and delivered them to my doorstep because you knew I didn't have the energy to talk. You took me for walks and helped me climb mountains. You brought me scarves and told me I was beautiful. You invited my voice, wanting to know the small moments that make a day worth living. May this long chant of *thank you* find its way into your hearts. May you know that what was given was received, deeply and completely.

To Priya Huffman, dear friend throughout the years of making this book: you were my eyes and ears when I went blind and deaf.

To Thomas Huffman, for your extraordinary love of learning. Thank you for the nudge.

To Fleur Green, for all the years traveling the inner waterways together with abiding love and outrageous humor. To Harvey Stone, for defining male friendship. You both held the lantern when all went dark.

To Nick Karaberis, the sentry, the gardener, and my friend, who brings all he touches to life. Every gift of your kindness made it possible for me to retreat to write.

To Paulette Fire: true to your name, you showed me where my fire was still lit. I couldn't have risen without you.

To Colt Prehm, painter, illustrator, and friend: thank you for your love of the human body. Your talent raised each part of the body to a greater love and appreciation. Thank you for being my ally when I was totally clueless in drawing class.

Max Regan, mentor, friend, fellow traveler, and my harbor: thank you for all the years of writing. I have never met anyone more talented, more generous, and more courageous. You touched every word of this book. It would not exist without you. Lisa Birman, Australian beauty: your gifts as a writer made this book sing.

Thank you to all the teachers and clients who have held me to the ground. You have widened and deepened my compassion. You have taught me to listen and to wait. You showed me that, at the end of the day, it is less about the fact that "bad things happen" but more about how we are with those "bad" things.

To all of you who have lost parts of your body, especially the women who have lost breasts: this is a club we never wanted to be part of. I wrote every page for all of us. My experience is simply mine and never would I assume it is yours. Thank you for your bravery; may we all redefine what it means to be whole.

To Gene Gollogly, publisher of Lantern Books, for staying up all night reading my manuscript and believing that it was more than one woman's story. To dear friends, David and Lila Tresemer for handing my manuscript to Gene and saying, "Don't ask. Just read this." To Martin Rowe, editor at Lantern: your fierce eye and intelligence made this a better book. Thank you for all your crisp feedback.

To Roger Jordan, for walking the walk as far as we could go. Your extraordinary ground made it possible for me to find home when the world tipped upside down. Thank you for more than I can say.

And finally, to my three children—Taylor, Cameron, and Brooke—there is but one strong and overwhelming *thank you*. By being exactly who you are, you kept calling me back to the well of life. Thank you for showing me exactly how big love can be.

GINNY JORDAN, MFA, is a writer, poet, and psychotherapist. She is co-founder of BeadforLife, a non-profit organization that works with women in Uganda to help them raise themselves out of poverty (beadforlife.org). Ginny has three children and has recently become a grandmother. She lives and works in Boulder, Colorado. For more on Ginny Jordan's work visit her website at ginny-jordan.com.